Dearest Michael

how can ye[...] [...]
here Today yoo [...]
You've Always [...] special To me,
I Think of yoo with much love
And pride in who yoo Are As a
person, husband And fAther - I
Admire yoor inTegrity. It is
difficult in these days to be...
remain A person of integrity.
My prayer for yoor birthday -
"May God who began the good
work within you (mike) keep right
on helping you grow in His grace
until His task within you is
finally finished on that day
...." Phillipians 1:6 + Living Bible
It has been a joyous experience
to be your older sister - even
when we couldn't get your jacket
off you in 98° temperature and
even when you would scare

IN THE CLEFT OF THE ROCK

John Charles Kerr

THOMAS NELSON
Nashville

Published in Nashville, Tennessee, by Thomas Nelson, Inc., and distributed in Canada by Lawson Falle, Ltd., Cambridge, Ontario.

Scripture quotations are from THE NEW KING JAMES VERSION. Copyright © 1979, 1980, 1982, Thomas Nelson, Inc., Publishers.

Scripture quotations noted NASV are from THE NEW AMERICAN STANDARD BIBLE. Copyright © 1960, 1962, 1963, 1968, 1971, 1972, 1973, 1975, 1977, by The Lockman Foundation and are used by permission.

Scripture quotations noted RSV are from the REVISED STANDARD VERSION of the Bible. Copyright © 1946, 1952, 1971, 1973 by the Division of Christian Education of the National Council of the Churches of Christ in the U.S.A. Used by permission.

Scripture quotations noted NIV are from the Holy Bible: NEW INTERNATIONAL VERSION. Copyright © 1978 by the New York International Bible Society. Used by permission of Zondervan Bible Publishers.

Original previously unpublished printing by E. Howard Kerr is published by permission of the E. Howard Kerr estate.

Library of Congress Cataloging-in-Publication Data

Kerr, John Charles.
    In the cleft of the rock / John Charles Kerr.
       p.   cm.
    Includes bibliographical references.
    ISBN 0-8407-3348-8
    1. Consolation.   2. Christian life—1960– I. Title.
BV4905.2.K47   1991
248.4—dc20   91-38971
                                    CIP

Printed in the United States of America

1 2 3 4 5 6 7 — 97 96 95 94 93 92

To my father, E. Howard Kerr,
whose creative, adventurous life
provided us with the richest shelter.

Preface

If this book is a confession of sorts that I am "sheltering" more than ever, an introductory explanation might be in order. I distinguish sheltering from escapism in that it takes place in the midst of life. Most of the material of *In the Cleft of the Rock* is built around forts and retreats that have been important to me for as long as I can remember. But almost all of them stand in the midst of the tumultuous activities of life, from the small-scale, snow-ball-laden gang warfare of boyhood to the pell-mell university world of the sixties, to the complexities of present professional days. Thus they offer, I think, possibilities of shelter that are very accessible for even the busiest of us, be it in a luncheon date or the use of a library. This book argues that we must shelter more, and that we must do it more profoundly. But we do not have to drop out in the process. I try to provide some practical help for lifestyles that are more up-tempo than mine.

Another distinction from mere escapism is that sheltering has to do with running *to* something rather than *from*. And the object pursued has much to do with the physical realities I call forts. No doubt we all have our tastes in forts. But to find the setting that provides rich shelter for you and to make that your center somehow—this is the primary concern here. In V. S. Naipaul's superb modern novel of shelter, *A House for Mr. Biswas,* the hero recovers from a nervous breakdown in an old Trinidadian estate home that is this kind of fortress:

> He remained in the Blue Room, feeling secure to be only a part of Hanuman House, an organism that possessed a life, strength and power to comfort which was quite separate from the individuals who composed it.[1]

Another defense one might make of sheltering is that it does strengthen us to reenter the fray. I see it in the tradition of the Desert Fathers who have become curious objects of admiration in our harried times. They "fled the world" in order to build a raft of sorts from which they could pull others to safety from the deluge of materialism they saw around them. Perhaps there is something of that in sheltering, though I do not like to overstate its utilitarian aspect by saying that "it makes you more effective." I feel about shelter the way Josef Pieper feels about leisure. He says, "No one who looks to leisure simply to restore his working powers will ever discover the fruit of leisure, he will never know the quickening that follows, almost as though from some deep sleep."[2]

So much for "sheltering" my flanks. My only other concern is that this matter of sheltering in "forts" may be taken too lightly, as so much child's play. I feel it important to add a note of urgency that may not come out in the book itself. It has to do with the increasing alienation that people of faith sense with our industrialized societies. This goes beyond what Peter's New Testament letter alludes to in calling Christians "aliens and strangers." God's people have always tended to see themselves that way, in the tradition of Abraham, the father of the faithful, who "obeyed and went, even though he did not know where he was going" and "made his home in the promised land like a stranger in a foreign country" (Heb. 11:8–9 NIV). People of faith live with a certain sense of alienation in that their primary concerns are otherwordly.

Nor is the alienation behind *In the Cleft of the Rock* a matter of coping with a culture that has turned hostile to faith. That, too, was the context of Peter's letter, likely written on the eve of Nero's persecution. We understand the increased evidence of hostility to people of faith in our Western industrialized societies. It is the intolerance of a culture that will tolerate almost anything except absolutes. This is oft-observed. This culture does not tolerate very well people of conviction, who say there is a moral code that should govern us all. Morality has gotten so internalized and subjective, we have almost no criteria for the rightness or wrongness of anything. In such a world, people of faith and strong conviction feel increasingly alienated.

Rather, my concern is alienation caused by change. "Future shock" is a very real phenomenon. When you take the factors that already make for alienation and add to them an accelerating engine of change that seems out of control, you have a very strong impulse to withdraw from the fray and find some shelter. Novelty, diversity, transience, impermanence—the social scientists look at these rumbling eruptions of change and advocate shelter for survival.

Our newspaper carried a recent article on "Twentieth Century Disease" that I thought put the matter concisely. Some people cannot cope with the postindustrial revolution, and their reaction is physical. The article cites a woman who these days can barely get out of bed. She is the victim of "a bizarre, poorly understood condition known as multiple chemical sensitivity." For reasons that modern science cannot quite explain, she is unable to tolerate even the lower levels of chemicals contained in the air and most everyday items. Sometimes called environmental illness, MCS continues to spawn controversy. Some doctors denounce it as nothing more than hocus-pocus, and those stricken often face a disheartening struggle for recognition of their condition as a legitimate illness. But for the victims, who endure a grim prison-like existence cut off from normal pursuits, diets restricted to a few organically-grown products, and bodies racked with pain, there is no question about the reality of the disorder. The antiseptic environments provided for these victims do not yet offer treatment and healing. They are more of a holding station, it seems, until more is learned. But they do express the urgency some people feel in finding ways to cope with modern living.

A true fort, on the other hand, enriches life immeasurably. The title of this book is drawn from the passages in Exodus where the Lord placed Moses in a cleft of a rock and covered him with his hand until he passed by. Moses saw his back, but not his face. Still, it was a supreme moment of revelation, the first self-disclosure of God in Scripture, proclaiming attributes that are drawn upon centuries later. What greater endorsement could there be for sheltering? God himself places people there so as to reveal himself to them more fully.

Contents

Part 1

A Pressing Need
for Shelter

Chapter 1

Give Me Shelter!

Back in Ottawa, in the fifties, we used to build snow forts. We would shovel the snow off the garage roof and make a good mountain to work with, or we waited for the street cleaners to stack it in the front yard with their long-chute snow blowers. We would whack it with the back of a shovel and give it a couple of days, and we'd have our raw material. We would dig straight in with a central tunnel, then start heading up in the middle for the lookout at the top. Once we had the basic layout, we hollowed it out carefully and iced it up inside and out—a little freezing rain always helped— so it was really strong. Then we had a fort. If things got too crazy around the house, we would grab some peanut butter sandwiches, always best semi-frozen anyway, and move outside: a private retreat . . . our fort. I remember lying in its interior darkness, pressing against its icy sides, touching the walls with the tip of my tongue. Our fort was our friend. We lined up snowballs around the lookout so everyone knew we could defend our fort if we had to.

Just recently, I dug myself out of another fort, a grand old hotel in the mountains, complete with a fairly private reading room. It shouldn't have surprised me, I suppose, to learn that twenty-five years after my childhood, forts are still important to me. The fact that men's toys are more expensive must not be the only difference between men and boys. Men's forts are also more elaborate, and maybe a little less satisfying. Anyway, when I got up to leave, I felt like I was digging up beets with my old gardener friend, pulling them out of the warm rich soil and shaking them off, throwing them in a cardboard box. I wanted to stay.

I thought about how often I keep returning, not to my grand old friend in the mountains necessarily, but to other hideaways: studies, cubicles, retreat centers, dining rooms. I saw clearly what I must have suspected earlier: my need for shelter seems to be getting stronger with the years. But how strange that I should need refuge now, of all times, when I'm not threatened or traumatized, really, in my comfortable suburban world. Why?

Insight came from prophetic voices. One voice is Alvin Toffler, a futurist at least, who says in *Future Shock*[1] that private enclaves will be increasingly important to us as the century draws to a close. In fact he says the trauma of our times is such, what with the future invading, the impermanence of things, our perpetual motion, that we need shelter more than ever. According to Toffler the very rate of change around us produces stress that makes it difficult to function effectively.

> There are discoverable limits to the amount of change that the human organism can absorb. . . . By endlessly accelerating change without first determining these limits, we may submit masses of men to demands they simply cannot tolerate.[2]

I begin to feel I am live evidence, especially when Toffler proposes forts, of sorts, to help.

> No society racing through the turbulence of the next several decades will be able to do without specialized centers in which the rate of change is artificially depressed. To phrase it differently, we shall need enclaves of the past—communities in which turnover, novelty and choice are deliberately limited. . . . In such slow-paced communities, individuals who need or want a more relaxed, less stimulating existence should be able to find it. The communities must be encapsulated, selectively cut off from the surrounding society.[3]

Old Testament Isaiah was a prophet of another traumatized generation. I am like "a polished arrow in a quiver," he said in one of the most appealing images of shelter I have found. We are "like a garden enclosed by a wall." The man's shelter metaphors are rich illustrations of what I desire: a spouse, forts, shade. It seems this need for shelter in the broad sense is universal. I was prepared to concede the point that "me" has become the sacred temple in our narcissistic times, that we are too self-absorbed as a generation and need a cause beyond ourselves to be truly fulfilled. But that does not preclude the need for shelter. In fact from what I was hearing, it is the very people most committed to causes outside themselves that most urgently face the question: How do we build a sense of personal shelter in volatile times? Where are the walls and coverings available to us all, we the strangers on the shore, pummeled and scattered by the "third wave"? Unless we have that, we will have little enough to offer any cause. My forts past and present hardly provided the answer to such pressing questions. But I do know one thing instinctively: Exposure can kill you.

Chapter 2

Exposure Kills

One day my snow fort was the last thing I needed. I was looking for much warmer shelter. I had stayed too long at Elgin Street School's outdoor rink with my ten-year-old friends: John Purcell, a tall, gangly kid with a wonderful fluid stride who seemed to have been born on skates, and Richard Berry, a darting center who could stickhandle through a thick crowd and always come out with the puck. There was a kid named Alfred who had taken a puck on the forehead in a recent game. I remember as though in slow motion, the blood beginning to appear through the square red mark and trickling down. And then there were the rest of us, the plodders, the guys who lined up along the boards and waited forever to be picked, the ones today's hockey coaches call "the players," a term that is the ultimate put-down. They needed us, though, just as slalom skiers need pylons. Without us there would be no game.

My skates must have been too small. I sat in the old changing room shack trying to rub my feet back to life, dreading the rush of pain as blood began to pour through frozen capillaries again. But I was still cold, even with my boots on and my feet starting to feel like they belonged to me again. Then I had about five blocks to walk home. Skates and hockey stick over one shoulder, arms full of old leather hockey gloves, books, and pads—I was so overloaded, and the weather so bitterly cold, I began to despair of ever being warm again. I was bawling loudly as I rounded our corner. A man who worked in the funeral home down the street from our house stepped out to give me a hand. He had red hair, a big, black overcoat, and a silk scarf. How could he look so neat and unaffected by the elements, as though he were not even aware that a new ice age had set in?

"I just have too much stuff!" I blubbered. He took a generous share and escorted me the last half block home.

I was so cold that later I had no trouble believing a news story of a young guy who died of exposure. He was a teenager who decided to walk the four miles from a northern town to his friend's place, as he had done often. But this time it was thirty-five below and he wasn't dressed for it. The elements got him.

Emotional exposure can kill you too. This is the essence of your most painful memories: that college year when you were utterly miserable with no hideaway and dorm life so intensely public; a lumber camp on the north shore of Lake Superior the following summer where you tried to recapture the fragments of an identity, seeking shelter as much as income.

I was sixteen. I remember standing around a summer camp truck shop with fifty teens. Just off the plane that day from Argentina, I was a missionary kid in culture shock.

"What's the matter with you?" asked the beautiful, tall, incredibly polished young woman at the counter, no trace of concern in the flash of her steel-blue eyes. "I remember you as a fun little kid!" That day I wasn't having fun.

We all live in culture shock, according to Alvin Toffler. The rate of change is so drastic, it is as though we are transplanted in history. Nothing seems familiar. We don't feel at home. Call it *future shock*.

EXPOSED

Well, when you run for as much shelter as I do, you say it must be true: we must be in a new kind of exposure. We must live with levels of transience, novelty, and diversity that are just too high. I think we *do* face change with growing weariness and wariness. We deal with adaptational breakdown; we may even be tampering with the emotional stability of humanity. When Toffler sums up by stating that "we long for a predictable environment"[1] and are in trouble without one, I look about my favorite fortress and think, but, of course!

THREATENED

Looking at the big picture, Toffler says we are really threatened today by the rumblings of change that will affect everything. Technology is the growling engine of change and exploding knowledge is its fuel. It is coming upon us so fast that we can't help but feel its influence in the transience of our relationships with people and things, places and ideas. "Transience . . . the forcible abbreviation of man's relationships, is not merely a condition of the external world. It has its shadow within us as well. New discoveries . . . erupt into our lives."[2] At the same time we have to cope with a flow of novelty and diversity unequaled in history. "We are simultaneously experiencing a youth revolution, a sexual revolution, a racial revolution, a colonial revolution, an economic revolution, and the most rapid . . . technological revolution in history."[3] The result is the "crisis of adaptation" which Toffler calls *future shock:* "We create an environment so ephemeral, unfamiliar, and complex as to threaten millions with adaptive breakdown."[4] Ours is a revolution so fundamental, say the historians, that we must search centuries past for a parallel. One such parallel is ancient Judah and its prophet Isaiah.

Exposure can kill you, and there is only one hiding place that can shelter you. This was Isaiah's message to his threatened nation in 730 B.C. A century of Assyrian weakness was over. A series of four mighty emperors was bursting on the scene in the empire with a homeland along the Tigris River in what is now northern Iraq: Tiglath-pileser, known as Pul in 2 Kings 15:19 (745–727 B.C.), Shelmaneser (727–721 B.C.), Sargon (721–705 B.C.), and Sennacharib (705–682 B.C.). Assyria was emerging as a superpower and some little neighbors were going to feel the heat!

What angered a youthful, cultured Isaiah and made him go public was a treaty agreed to about 730 B.C. between Judah and Assyria. Little Judah was threatened by two lesser neighbors to the north and needed help, but Isaiah was convinced that making a deal with Assyria was hardly looking for help in the right place. As John Oswalt says, it was like "a mouse paying a cat for help against another mouse."[5] Isaiah saw the danger of Judah getting gobbled up in the process, so he lectured King Ahaz about his lack of faith: "Take care, and be calm, have no fear and do not be fainthearted because of these two stubs of smoldering firebrands. . . . If you will not believe, you surely shall not last" (Isa. 7:4, 9 NASV). The confederacy he feared so much was of two nations in decline. Within a few short years they would be off the world scene completely. On the other hand, Assyria was the rising world power. It would soon overrun all its southern neighbors and have Judah by the throat. Why encourage mighty Assyria to do what it was going to do anyway?

Sure enough Assyria did sweep down during Isaiah's time in a show of power that established it beyond doubt as the superpower of its day. The prophet described the invasion: "They shall come with speed, swiftly. No one will be weary or stumble among them" (Isa. 5:26–27). Under Tiglath-pileser the mighty army pushed southward, extracting immediate tribute from Menahem, king of Israel (see 2 Kings 15:19), before 731 B.C. King Ahaz was left with no illusions about where the real power lay as he stood in the ruins of Damascus and was forced to enter a binding treaty with Assyria and recognize its deities (see 2 Kings 16:10–16 and 2 Chron. 28:20–21).

Shalmaneser followed and by the year 724 had laid siege to Samaria, Israel's capital city. It took his army three years to starve the city into submission, but siege warfare prevailed. Judah's northern cousins fell to Assyria in 721, leaving behind a tiny kingdom to the south that was extremely vulnerable.

Under Sargon, the Assyrian superpower reached the height of its dominance. There was a decisive victory over a northern neighbor called Urartu in 714 and over Merodach-baladan of Babylon in 710. In every direction Assyria's enemies lay crushed. Sargon became known as "lord of the universe." His overweening pride was not unlike that described in Isaiah 14:13-14:

> *You said in your heart,*
> *"I will ascend to heaven;*
> *I will raise my throne above the stars of God,*
> *And I will sit on the mount of assembly*
> *In the recesses of the north.*
> *I will ascend above the heights of the clouds;*
> *I will make myself like the Most High."* (NASV)

Sennacharib was barely established as Sargon's successor when he had Jerusalem surrounded. Flooding south, Assyria overthrew the coast city of Tyre and the Philistine cities of Ekron and Ashkelon. Judah's frontier fortress, Lachish, was put under siege and Rabshakeh was dispatched to Jerusalem with the ultimatum, "Where are the gods of Hamath and Arpad? Where are the gods of Sepharvaim? And when have they delivered Samaria from my hand? Who among all the gods of these lands have delivered their land from my hand, that the Lord should deliver Jerusalem from my hand?" (Isa. 36:19-20 NASV).

TRAUMATIZED

The kind of trauma our generation faces is, according to Toffler, a "form of personality maladjustment which is a reaction to an unsuccessful attempt to adjust to new surroundings and people." In its most extreme form this maladjustment makes communication next to impossible, gives a distorted picture of reality, and causes a kind of inertia. Toffler compares it to the trauma of soldiers who are driven to the limits of adaptability in battle. He cites instances of "long range penetration strain" where soldiers will surrender to an overpowering apathy and fall asleep in the midst of battle. Similarly, victims of natural disasters are sometimes "reduced to total confusion and mindlessness . . . incapable of the most elementary rational decision-making."[6]

Such experiences, he says, will be widely shared by coming

generations faced with rapid change where familiar objects and relationships are gone. Confusion, disorientation, fatigue, and anxiety, even that "point of no return" where apathy and emotional withdrawal set in—can any of us say such symptoms are foreign to us?

Toffler's "point of no return" reminds us just how vital emotional shelter is. Like the culturally-shocked person, we know what psychologist Sven Lundstedt calls a "subjective feeling of loss, a sense of isolation and loneliness." We long for an environment which is "predictable and less uncertain."[7] We need, in short, a fort.

In Isaiah's time, the pressure of Assyria on Judah was compounded by its atrocities. Consequently Judah became one of the most traumatized nations in history. Israel to the north had been literally starved out under Sennacharib. True, the prophets had predicted a downfall some fifty years earlier: "An adversary shall surround the land, and bring down your defenses from you and your strongholds shall be plundered" (Amos 3:11 RSV). But who would have believed the horrors of a four-year siege like the one described in 2 Kings 6:25? "There was a great famine in Samaria; and behold they besieged it until a donkey's head was sold for eighty shekels of silver, and a fourth of a kab of dove's dung for five shekels of silver" (NASV). The horror was so great that one woman said to another, "Give your son that we may eat him today, and we will eat my son tomorrow" (2 Kings 6:28).

We catch the desperation in the conversation between four lepers at the gates of a besieged Jerusalem: "Why do we sit here until we die? If we say, 'We will enter the city,' then the famine is in the city and we shall die there; and if we sit here, we die also. . . . Let us go over to the camp of the Arameans" (2 Kings 7:3-4). Similar measures were advocated to Judah by Jeremiah when Jerusalem was in the last stages of the Assyrian siege. To remain in the city was to perish by famine, pestilence, or sword. But to walk out and surrender was to survive (see Jer. 38:18).

Meanwhile, traumatized Judah, a tiny kingdom under a series of vacillating kings, remained on its land. The only real leader was their eloquent and fearless prophet, Isaiah. No wonder he spoke often of refuge to these people. The transience of their lives made them feel threatened. The emotional instability of their society was in such disarray, they must have needed refuge as much as any society in history. It was not a time, Isaiah argued, to be pro- or anti-Assyrian. Greater alliances would be needed if they were to survive. Only a sense of spiritual shelter could possibly help. Isaiah's traumatized people needed God.

DEFEATED

Prophets do have a way of dealing with doom. In much the same way Isaiah spoke of doom to his people, Toffler leaves no doubt that the storm of late twentieth century change will leave many victims in its wake. He describes the escapism of the young Americans who live in seaside caves on Crete, having given up any further effort to cope with the exploding high-speed complexities of life.[8] He calls them early victims of future shock. And he includes a good deal more of their countrymen when he speaks of the escape sought in drugs, a video-induced stupor, an alcoholic haze, flight from parental and work responsibilities, tranquilizers, and psychic pacifiers. "Affluence makes it possible, for the first time in history, for large numbers of people to make their withdrawal a full-time proposition . . . [a] total surrender before the strain of decision-making in conditions of uncertainty and overchoice."[9] Many respond to the complexities of modern industrial society by denial, specialism, and reversion—techniques that "will only deepen . . . adaptive difficulties."[10] In times like these, we all deal with escapist tendencies which cannot provide the true shelter we need. There must be something more.

Isaiah saw clearly that his nation would get trampled. In fact, a good part of his message was directed to a later generation which had already fallen. Not only was a nation *exposed, threatened,* and *traumatized,* it was *defeated.* Jerusalem had clearly fallen and it was time to speak of comfort and regathering. This was "a people robbed and plundered" (Isa. 42:22). Whether later authors were needed to speak precisely about a regathering of Israel under Cyrus the Mede some 200 years after Isaiah's time (see Isa. 45), or whether Isaiah himself saw the future in detail, is left largely to one's view of inspiration and bibliology. The reason why many scholars posit at least two Isaiahs is the obvious change at Isaiah 40. However, I find it interesting to think that Isaiah's prophetic powers were such that he could grasp his nation's future as well as its past and present. He would have been able to offer shelter to his people not only when they were threatened and traumatized, but when they were actually defeated. A place to nurse their wounds, to gain respite, to be free to recover an identity—that is the refuge Isaiah holds out in the latter part of his book.

Exposed, threatened, traumatized, defeated, such words describe all of us world citizens as we race toward the twenty-first century. Our prophets are agreed on the dangers. And they map out strategies for survival that involve decisive action and personal stability zones. While running is an option, it certainly is not the answer. We need to meet invention with invention. We need something like Isaiah's place, "like a polished arrow in a quiver." We need a place that is hidden, but useful.

Chapter 3

False Shelter Is Like a Buckled Wall

Suddenly the sky was so black it convinced even the most fanatic golfers to head for cover. The weather had been spotty all day, with patches of sunshine amid squalls. But this was more serious. Streaks of chain lightning cut through the black sky. My partner and I charged off a green and headed for a shack in the woods. It was clearly no longer in use but there it was. In a lightning storm it looked very inviting. It was already raining steadily by the time we got there and ducked inside.

We heard later that a man was killed in that storm not far from where we were—not a golfer, but a roofer. He was struck by lightning. So our little shelter may have done some good. But it certainly didn't keep us dry! There was a time in there, with the wind whipping rain through the walls and several small rivers pouring down through the roof, that we wondered if we might not have kept drier outside. But by then huge hailstones were beating on our barn boards and we dared not move.

We emerged like a pair of Noah's shaky birds, delighted to be walking on freshly washed sod with bright hailstones the size of golf balls lying all around, and thoroughly drenched. The clubhouse sent out rescue carts to get people off the course. Golf was over for the day.

Like the shack in the woods where my friend and I took refuge from the storm, sometimes coverage is just plain inadequate. We can, for example, forge relationships that cost us everything and deliver very little in return such as thinking that two halves in marriage make a whole. It takes two whole people to make one strong marriage. When one partner pays dearly for the relationship and receives nothing in return, there is little true shelter involved. Far from offering emotional shelter, some relationships are more dangerous than back alleys. Yet, abusive relationships, like cracked walls about to collapse, have enough of the veneer of the shelter of "home" about them that they keep many people hanging on far too long. What battered wives tell us is that we have a huge need for the shelter of home and family. As Alvin Toffler says, the family is the "giant shock absorber" of society, "the one stable point in an increasingly flux-filled environment." But as the superindustrial revolution unfolds, this shock absorber will "come in for some shocks of its own."[1]

Some jobs are little more than a shelter against poverty. These too can cost us dearly, delivering little more than a paycheck. According to *Psychology Today,* many of us are "bored to sickness" by our work.[2] My local newspaper recently told of a thirty-eight-year-old father of four who spends forty-eight hours a week on an assembly line stapling, then lifting fifty-seven car seats per hour. The job has treated him well financially, but he wakes up mornings filled with a nameless dread. At night he collapses in front of the TV, a nervous, exhausted heap. His job is costing him more than he realizes—and not delivering enough in return.

Security on the deepest level does not come to us through family and work alone. Even at their best, these great bastions cannot consistently deliver the level of security we need. Strangely, surrounding ourselves with people does not seem to work much better. There must be, we say, some "strength in numbers." What we discover in the crowd, however, is a somber truth: Not only does the crowd fail to provide the nurturing environment we expect, it actually precludes it. The worst loneliness of all, we learn, is the one we experience in the press of humanity.

Philip Carey, a character in *Of Human Bondage,* joins all of Paris in the pursuit of emotional shelter:

> It was cold and windswept. People hurried by wrapped up in their coats, shrunk together in an effort to keep out of the cold, and their faces were pinched and careworn. . . . Philip felt lonely in the world and strangely homesick. He wanted company.[3]

Instinctively, he reaches out to an American friend named Flanagan and the two end up at the Bal Bullier. But the gregarious Flanagan disappears and Philip is left alone again, watching the dancers. His vision becomes Somerset Maugham's eloquent commentary on humanity's desperate flight from loneliness and a private "world of horror":

> The hall was lit with great white lights, low down, which emphasized the shadows on the faces; all the lines seemed to harden under it, and the colours were most crude. It was a sordid scene. Philip leaned over the rail, staring down. . . . It seemed to Philip that they had thrown off the guard which people wear on their expression, the homage to convention, and he saw them now as they really were. In that moment of abandon they were strangely animal. . . . They danced furiously as though impelled by some strange power within them, and it seemed to Philip that they were driven forward by a rage for enjoyment. They were seeking desperately to escape from a world of horror. The desire for pleasure . . . urged them blindly on, and the very vehemence of the desire seemed to rob it of all pleasure. . . . They danced as though everlasting darkness were beneath their feet.[4]

When Philip Carey grabs his coat and goes out into the bitter night, we feel the vanity of this pursuit. His loneliness, like ours, is an inner emptiness that is simply not filled by crowds.

On the contrary, when we read Isaiah's words we discover how to fill the emptiness. He said, "In returning and rest, quietness and trust" there is strength (see Isa. 30:15). Solitude provides the means of inner growth which fortifies us internally. Strangely enough, people can feel most inwardly fortified at the very times they are most physically cut off. Anne Morrow Lindbergh describes the process in *Gift From the Sea:*

> It is not physical solitude that actually separates one from other men, not physical isolation, but spiritual isolation. It is not the desert island nor the stony wilderness that cuts you from the people you love. It is the wilderness in the mind, the desert wastes in the heart through which one wanders lost and a stranger. When one is a stranger to oneself then one is estranged from others too. If one is out of touch with oneself, then one cannot touch others. How often in a large city, shaking hands with my friends, I have felt the wilderness stretching between us. Both of us were wandering in arid wastes, having lost the springs that nourished us—or having found them dry. Only when one is connected to one's own core is one connected to others. . . . And for me, the core, the inner spring can best be refound through solitude.
>
> I walked far down the beach, soothed by the rhythm of the waves, the sun on my bare back and legs, the wind and mist from the spray on my hair. Into the waves and out like a sandpiper. And then home, drenched, drugged, reeling, full to the brim with my day alone; full like the moon before the night has taken a single nibble of it; full as a cup poured up to the lip.[5]

Be alone. Be still. Here is counsel that provides the least expensive and most accessible shelter available to us. Now that there are over five billion of us on the planet, it seems no small challenge. Yet, as Thomas à Kempis reminds us, this shelter may be as immediate as closing the door.

> No man is worthy of heavenly comfort, unless he have diligently exercised himself in holy compunction. If thou desirest true contrition of heart, enter into thy secret chamber, and shut out the tumults of the world. . . . Whoso therefore withdraweth himself from his acquaintance and friends, God will draw near unto him with his holy Angels. . . . Shut thy door upon thee, and call unto Jesus, thy Beloved. Stay with Him in thy closet; for thou shalt not find so great peace any where else.[6]

Strangely enough, Isaiah literally exposed himself for a time to get a similar message across:

> *In the year that the supreme commander, sent by Sargon king of Assyria, came to Ashdod and attacked and captured it—at that time the LORD spoke through Isaiah son of Amoz. He said to him, "Take off the sackcloth from your body and the sandals from your feet." And he did so, going around stripped and barefoot. Then the Lord said, "Just as my servant Isaiah has gone stripped and barefoot for three years, as a sign and portent against Egypt and Cush, so the king of Assyria will lead away stripped and barefoot the Egyptian captives and Cushite exiles, young and old, with buttocks bared—to Egypt's shame. Those who trusted in Cush and boasted in Egypt will be afraid and put to shame. In that day the people who live on this coast will say, 'See what has happened to those we relied on, those we fled to for help and deliverance from the king of Assyria! How then can we escape?'"* (Isa. 20:1–6 NIV)

Pretty extreme measures to make a point! The Hebrew word *ārôm* can be used to mean partial nudity, which in Isaiah's culture would have conveyed the message just as well. The outer garment of sackcloth, perhaps the customary dress of prophets, and the inner tunic would have been removed, leaving only the loincloth. Nor did the prophet necessarily go about this way for three years. The phrase "for three years it is a sign" could indicate the length of time to which the sign points. Still, such behavior was bizarre and offensive in Isaiah's society. He must have been very anxious to issue his warning. And there was good reason.

Ashdod, the northernmost of the five great Philistine cities which lay just thirty-three miles west of Jerusalem, had fallen to Sargon in 711. Its king had fled to Egypt only to find this refuge very weak indeed—they meekly handed him over to Assyria. So Isaiah is acting out a proven truth here: Egypt is no more reliable as a refuge for Judah than she was for Ashdod. Egypt itself would be led naked into captivity, as indeed it was some forty years later under Esarhaddon. Judah could no longer get away with looking to the south when relations to the north deteriorated. There was no refuge there. Egypt was just as exposed as anyone else.

This theme is picked up again in chapters 30 and 31 when Judah is probably *in extremis,* around 701. All of Hezekiah's hoped-for allies had proven unreliable. His revolt against Assyria was a shambles. His outer fortresses had fallen. The end was very much at hand. If any human help could be found, it had to be in Egypt! But the prophet confronted Hezekiah with a warning about false shelters:

> *"Woe to the rebellious children," says the Lord . . .*
> *"Who walk to go down to Egypt,*
> *And have not asked My advice . . .*
> *To strengthen themselves in the strength of Pharaoh,*
> *And to trust in the shadow of Egypt."* (Isa. 30:1–2)

This idea was especially offensive to Isaiah's God because Egypt was the very nation that had once enslaved Israel. They were expressly forbidden from going back there (see Ex. 13:17). Egypt might seem like a "refuge," "protection," "shelter," and "shadow," but such shelter would be Judah's shame (see v. 3). It was an illusion. In reality, Egypt was beyond being of much help to anyone. She was ruled by Shabako, a pharaoh who was not even truly Egyptian. Far from being able to protect anyone, Egypt could not even produce her own leadership.

Weak as they were, such shelters cost a bundle. To share Egypt's protection, the shelter seekers must cart their wealth on beasts through the Negev desert, a "land of trouble and anguish." All of this to go to a "people who cannot profit them," who sits there like an aged sea monster—"Rahab who sits still" (see Isa. 30:6–7 NASV). It is ironic that Judah was willing to pay dearly for such dubious protection when she already had the ultimate shelter, the "mountain of the Lord . . . the Rock of Israel" (30:29 NASV).

Rejecting their true God for Egypt was like hiding in the shadow of a shaky wall. Isaiah was very specific as he drew his image of a truly unreliable shelter:

> *This iniquity shall be to you*
> *Like a breach ready to fall,*
> *A bulge in a high wall,*
> *Whose breaking comes suddenly,*
>   *in an instant.* (Isa. 30:13)

This alliance would be so unreliable, Isaiah warned, it would end up smashed to smithereens, so ruthlessly shattered that "among its pieces not a fragment will be found for taking coals from a hearth or scooping water out of a cistern" (Isa. 30:14 NASV). Egypt is no hiding place. "He who helps will stumble, he who is helped will fall; both will perish together" (Isa. 31:3 NASV).

Tecpan, Guatemala is a little tin-roofed town in the shadows of some massive Maya ruins. The roofs of the houses seemed so lightweight and unattractive that we wondered why they had not been made of the beautiful red tile seen elsewhere in this land of eternal spring. When we asked, we heard the story of unreliable covering. Tecpan was devastated in the huge earthquake of 1978, which claimed some 14,000 lives. Hardly a household did not lose a family member. And the killer, in many cases, was the tile roof. Such was the force of the tremors that what looked like a sheltering roof became a cascading avalanche of deadly stone. Much better, they learned, to stand in the heaving streets than to take refuge beneath those tile roofs.

It seems that no shelter is better than false shelter. Isaiah calls on his generation to turn away from their frantic pursuits and find strength in stillness: "In quietness and confidence shall be your strength" (Isa. 30:15). It is not on the open plains in flight on "swift steeds" that true shelter can be found. These people could not outrun their pursuers. Without change, they would be left "as a pole on top of a mountain, and as a banner on a hill" (Isa. 30:17). It is hard to imagine a more exposed position than standing on the top of a mountain.

Mountaintop moments are great for pictures. We stood on the summit of 11,000-foot Big Sister last summer and just wanted to linger after the tough, four-hour climb. It was a supreme moment: watching the sun starting to drop toward Mount Assiniboine in the west; looking straight down two miles at the tiny houses around the town of Canmore; and staring across at twelve-thousand-foot Mount Lougheed. There is no greater feeling than sitting on top of the world that way. But look around you! The pure desolation of jagged rocks two hours above the tree line—is there the slightest urge to stay on such an exposed peak? Not even the most intrepid mountaineer wants to stay above the tree line after nightfall, even if going to higher heights next morning. To be left like a flagstaff on a mountain is the most desolate exposure I can imagine.

But what is real shelter? This is a theme that Isaiah explored in detail in times as traumatic as our own. Perhaps the nature of the times accounts for the appeal of his lovely shelter images. He did not just say, "Your only refuge is in God." Rather, his descriptions help us *feel* overshadowed by drawing pictures of the shelters available to us. A vital faith, he said, is like a garden wall, surrounding your life for the purposes of creativity and fruitfulness. There is the image of Jerusalem as mother: "On her sides shall you be carried, and be dandled on her knees" (Isa. 66:12). Having a sense of destiny is like being a polished arrow in a quiver. There is the sense of being upheld by a father's strong hands: "I will strengthen you, I will help you, I will uphold you with my victorious right hand" (Isa. 41:10 NASV). You are called "Like a woman forsaken and grieved in spirit, like a youthful wife of youth when you were refused. . . . For a mere moment I have forsaken you, but with great mercies I will gather you" (Isa. 54:6–7).

Such images cause us to feel "held." There are walls of protection, "In my house and within my walls a place and a name better than that of sons and daughters" (Isa. 56:5 NASV). There is the precious, refreshing shade of the east: "Like heat by the shadow of a cloud, the song of the ruthless is silenced" (Isa. 25:5 NASV). There is the "rock of your refuge" (Isa. 17:10 NASV). We feel the covering of a strong tent, "A tent which shall not be folded; its stakes shall never be pulled up, nor any of its cords be torn apart" (Isa. 33:20 NASV). We are sheltered as though hidden in the mountains or protected by a covenant and a strong ruler; we have the protection of strong gates (see Isa. 56). This nation is "covered" with clothing that does not wear out and the promise of a secure land and city: "For I will create Jerusalem to be a delight and its people a joy. I will rejoice over it and take delight in my people; the sound of weeping and of crying will be heard in it no more" (Isa. 65:18–19 NIV).

They have the place of rest where "the weary rest. . . . This is the place of repose" (Isa. 28:12 NIV). It is a place of peace, of property protected by a strong hedge, of sanctuary: "The Lord Almighty is the one you are to regard as holy. . . . He will be as a sanctuary" (Isa. 8:13–14 NIV). He is a fortress, a hiding place, a guard, a comforter, a covering, a shelter. "The Lord will create above every dwelling place of Mount Zion and above her assemblies a cloud and smoke by day and the shining of a flaming fire by night. For over all the glory there will be a covering. And there will be a tabernacle for shade in the daytime from the heat, for a place of refuge, and for a shelter from storm and rain" (Isa. 4:5–6).

Isaiah's metaphors describe what true shelter is really like. It has to do with the strength of personal relationships that give significance to our lives, the sense of being special. These are the images of the walled garden and of family members. Shelter also has to do with secret places, and for this we have the images of sealed rooms, the arrow in a quiver, burial beneath an ocean of knowledge. Then there is the shelter of ceremony contained in images of covenant, sanctuary, and clothing. Security is fundamental to a sense of shelter, as we see in the images of a secure tent, firm foundations, and strong mountains. Structure and order contribute to our sense of shelter. For this we have images of walls, doors, and gates. There is something about a shepherd or ruler that imparts a special dimension of shelter. And the idea of being shaded, covered, or overshadowed suggests another kind of protection.

Why is shelter important? Because it provides a sense of being special, of a secret place, of ceremony, of security, of structure, of being shepherded, and of being shaded. I suspect that my perception of a need for shelter and my pursuit of it in various ways is an expression of my recognition that such things matter much to me. When my shelter quotient is down, I seem to reach out for it instinctively.

The following pages are based on the assumption that our shelter needs are pressing because they have to do with our sense of significance, privacy, ceremony, security, structure, guidance, and protection. We will reflect upon these seven general categories of shelter, using Isaiah's images. How do we reach them, both physically and emotionally? Is there a larger, spiritual dimension where we find shelter in an ultimate, unbroken sense? We will explore some of my old forts again for helpful clues, and draw on the experience and insights of some fellow fort lovers.

Part 2

Shelter Means Feeling Special

The mountain fortress that got all this started is actually the Banff Springs Hotel, a massive stone structure of some 700 rooms at the juncture of the Spray and Bow rivers in a stunning stretch of the Canadian Rockies. You can sit at one of the huge arched windows, eight feet across by some twelve feet high, and watch tiny golfers work their way down the lush green strip of the second fairway, dots of color against the green and gray mass of 10,000-foot Mount Rundle hard against them. From my desk near the king-size fireplace, the broad face of Rundle is like a giant slab of pistachio ice cream with a rounded bite taken out of the top. At the right season, the hotel lobby is appropriately hushed beneath its sixteen-foot ceilings and chandeliers. Huge doors lead off into the Cascade dining room with its tantalizing aromas and the tinkle of china and silverware. Yes, a good fort is designed on a grand scale.

I have had others. There is the roof of the *Instituto Biblico Rio de La Plata* where I spent a good deal of my thirteenth year. It was flat and covered with tar and gravel. I reached it by a steel ladder up one wall off the balcony, which housed the water tanks. But all around the roof was a wall of turrets so one could fend off invading hordes, if necessary, with cannons. I flew my kites from that grand roof, launching the colored beauties made of bamboo cane well above the thick trees of the lush grounds below. And I looked down on all mortals, including the students who filtered out for walks among the trees between classes. Someone should have assigned me to catch truants! I remember spotting the fairest of them all one day, walking quietly alone, separated from me by some thirty feet and, even worse, an inexorable span of years.

"Hola!" I called.

She looked up with the mystified impatience of her more serious world. *Pero que haces ahi?* "What are you doing up there?" What indeed? I suppose I am still answering her question.

Elevation was an important part of these forts. There was my tree house in the Cobourg weeping willow, just in front of my parents' summer cottage. It was probably the least substantial of my grand forts, for I swayed in the wind among its highest limbs. But it had that essential ingredient of all ivory towers, elevation. Hard dirt roads, people, cottages, even the bulky dining hall across the way—I looked down on it all like a monarch. Looking south, I felt suspended over vast Lake Ontario, which stretched to the horizon. There have been other great trees: *nisperos* and figs in Argentina, which always supplied a choice snack in the late afternoon; towering eucalyptus trees that provided no easy access but great climbing once the first leap was made. But that willow was the one that kept calling me back. I knew its limbs so well that I could scale the thing from ground to summit in a flash.

Then there are the ivory towers I have frequented, such as Calgary Tower with its Olympic Flame up top, a remnant of the Winter Games of 1988. You'll find me there for an early breakfast, watching the sun rise over the infinite prairies and casting its warm glow on the dark forms of the Rocky Mountains in the West. The view seems to encompass half the continent. From there 11,000-foot Big Sister rises to prominence in its range along the horizon. I survey the foothills that lie between us, rolling and ridged in their evergreen garb, then the city up close with its mix of concrete and greenery. For all my visits, there are always new discoveries: a park I have not noticed, a trail I have not jogged. Like most of these revolving towers, you do a full circle in an hour and survey the whole city. There have been other towers, but never one I have enjoyed so much in early morning peace as Calgary Tower.

One thing I like in these lofty perches is the freedom to think big for a time, to not worry about the small details of life—all the nit-picking concerns for dollars and people that tend to pile up on one's doorstep daily. I can look at life "whole" and address it like a painter with bold, broad strokes on a fresh canvas. I need to climb an ivory tower on occasion and feel as though I am monarch of all I survey. A wonderful poem written long ago tells how that feels:

> "I am monarch of all I survey
>   My right there is none to dispute,
> From the center all round to the sea,
>   I am Lord of the fowl and the brute . . ."[1]

There is something about the superior vantage point these places offer. Running to them must have something to do with getting out of the trenches and seeing the overall picture. Perhaps it is related to an urge to develop a strategy, making the decisions that affect my life.

There is also a strong sense of transcendence in these lofty forts of mine. Looking down from a willow is much the same as looking down from some sparkling revolving tower: You have ascended above the grubbiness, the muck and disorder of life, and you look down on that (dare I say it?) with fairly lofty disdain. It's a very heady feeling. For instance, take the rather reclusive young hero of Willo Davis Roberts' *View From a Cherry Tree*. Here's a kid who is always passing judgment on all who dare venture beneath his tree: his sister's boyfriends, relatives, acquaintances, repairmen. To the boy in the tree they are all some lesser form of life. I understand perfectly his superior attitude in that lofty perch.

It may be a sense of being special that is fostered in certain lofty settings, the sense of having gifts and ideals that are unique in the world. No doubt we all need to feel that way about ourselves, what with the bombardment of things working to reduce us all to the level of the lowest common denominator. Parents can use their influence that way, the school system too. The right kind of fortress is a great help in nurturing the vital sense of being special.

This relates to my grand dining rooms with their tinkling silverware and heady aromas and white linen. They have a loftiness of spirit which puts them in the same class as my ivory towers. I occasionally choose to lunch at the elegant Trader's dining room in our town rather than the local dairy bar simply because they treat me like royalty at Trader's. I may pay perhaps twice the price of the dairy bar, but the experience nourishes the part of me that longs for C. S. Lewis-style aristocracy.

Because we need to cherish our uniqueness in lofty private enclaves from time to time, there must be something to finding our own ivory towers, places to preserve one's essence. Otherwise we live out the lives of others or be reduced to the level of a human ant, of prosaic barbarianism. Part of the answer may be as simple as eating out less often but doing it with elegance.

There is a third dimension to these kinds of forts, that of sheer reverie. I can identify at times with Ishmael on the masthead pursuing the great white whale in *Moby Dick:*

> In the serene weather of the tropics it is exceedingly pleasant—the mast-head; nay, to a dreamy meditative man it is delightful. There you stand, a hundred feet above the silent decks, striding long the deep, as if the masts were gigantic stilts, while beneath you and between your legs, as it were, swim the hugest monsters of the sea, even as ships once sailed between the boots of the famous Colossus at old Rhodes. There you stand, lost in the infinite series of the sea, with nothing ruffled but the waves. The tranced ship indolently rolls; the drowsy trade winds blow; everything resolves you into languor. For the most part, in this tropic whaling life, a sublime uneventfulness invests you; you hear no news; read no gazettes; extras with startling accounts of commonplaces never delude you into unnecessary excitements; you hear of no domestic afflictions; bankrupt securities; fall of stocks; are never troubled with the thought of what you shall

have for dinner—for all your meals for three years and more are snugly stowed in casks, and your bill of fare is immutable.[2]

Ishmael's perch sounds a lot like Alvin Toffler's "enclaves of the past" with its isolation from the news.

Sheer reverie is a very vital part of any good retreat center. If it is nice to see the large picture and feel that you have risen above the ordinary, it is delightful to lose yourself for a time in the mystical pleasures of an ivory tower. You can drift away in this atmosphere, quite forgetting that there are parking meters, deadlines, and the like. Time ceases to be, and in my best moments I am more a part of eternity.

Probably what we indulge in at such times is what Roger von Oech calls "soft thinking." In *A Whack on the Side of the Head: How to Unlock Your Mind for Innovation*, Von Oech describes "soft thinking" as metaphorical, approximate, humorous, playful. "Hard thinking" on the other hand is more logical, precise, specific, and consistent. If hard thinking is like a spotlight in its intensity, soft thinking is more like a floodlight, more diffuse and covering a wider area. Soft thinking is crucial in creativity:

> Both types of thinking play an important role in the creative process, but usually during different phases. Soft thinking is quite effective in the germinal phase when you are searching for new ideas, thinking globally and manipulating problems. Hard thinking, on the other hand, is best used in the practical phase.[3]

Von Oech reminds us that unfortunately our soft thinking skills are poorly developed by our educational system. Indeed, we train our children to eliminate soft thinking, or at best see it as relatively insignificant. He shows us that the mind is not only a computer that processes information, but is also a museum that stores experiences and a playground in which to play.

It is crucial that we not dismiss our ivory towers as so much time-wasting escapism. We need to "scale the utmost height," whether it be to a dining room, library, or some other more precarious perch. You can rise above things in your mind. I find some kind of physical ascent a great stimulus for the mind to follow suit.

Von Oech has a simple exercise to help stimulate metaphorical thinking. You start with "life is like" and fill in the rest. One of his metaphors likens life to a banana: "You start out green and get soft and mushy with age. Some people want to be one of the bunch while others want to be top banana. You have to take care not to slip on externals. And finally, you have to strip off the outer coating to get at the meat."[4]

My favorite is, "Life is like riding an elevator. It has a lot of ups and downs and someone is always pushing your buttons. Sometimes you get the shaft, but what really bothers you are the jerks."[5]

I like to think the elevator also leads up to that "soft" environment of a lofty fort, where creative ideas are born.

Chapter 4

Like a Held Child

Snow forts have their limitations. They're a handy getaway when you need some coolish privacy. But when you have real trouble, like when you've been caught wrestling in the school gym instead of being in the auditorium at choir practice and may, so everyone agrees, be kicked out of school, the place to run is home. Or when Georgie Dunn, the kid with the fastest fists in the school, is after you; or when your ball has shattered Mrs. Wilson's window and you don't dare face her alone; or when you have been discovered drawing indecencies in art and this time, for sure, you are history—at such critical moments, the only place to run is home.

The indecency charge was the one that really made me appreciate my home base. It was a horrible thing to be eleven years old and caught pen in hand, "flagrante delicto" you could say, sketching vulgarities. My world crashed in. All was discovered. I ran home and told my mother, through bitter tears, "And . . . and . . . I'm going to be kicked out of school!" The world had ended. I will never forget the miracle as she assimilated this desperate news, pondered it a moment, and resolved the problem with adult dispatch. Yes, my mother heard the sordid tale without reproach, hugged me and soaked up my tears. Father was called in for some somber discussion and prayer; an interview was arranged with Mr. Henry, the principal, in which it was agreed to remove some copies of *National Geographic* which were deemed lewd. In short, my life in the community was salvaged with minimal disgrace. It was a miracle!

How school kids survive without the refuge of home has been a mystery to me ever since. I have no trouble believing the horror stories of boarding school life described by C. S. Lewis and Anthony Trollope. Trollope's experience was especially miserable because of his poverty and attendance as a day student. His confirmed hopelessness is that of a miserable student who lacks the refuge of a loving home:

> I was again sent to that school as a day-boarder. . . . Perhaps the eighteen months which I passed in this condition, walking to and fro on those miserably dirty lanes, was the worst period of my life. I was now over fifteen, and had come to . . . appreciate at its full the misery of expulsion from all social intercourse. . . . There was a parlour in which my father lived, shut up among big books; but I passed my hours in the kitchen; it all added to the cruelty of the days. . . . The indignities I endured are not to be described. As I look back it seems to me that all hands were against me,—those of the masters as well as boys."[1]

Incredibly enough, home is the *place* of obscenity for many of today's children. What would I ever have done, I ask, if I had been running *from* home rather than *to* it in my eleven-year-old world? Bearing my disgrace alone, forced to squeeze out what solace I could amid the severity and distortions of other people—what *would* I have done? Or if home had not been a place of unqualified acceptance, where I could unburden myself without recrimination—would I not have been condemned to bearing my sins alone, to face the austere judge, Mr. Henry, in the most dreadful overexposure?

It seems almost trite to tell other offenders like me that God can hold you when other arms have failed. Yet this is the familiar expression of the Psalms: "When my father and my mother forsake me, then the LORD will take care of me" (Ps. 27:10). This theme is picked up by Isaiah in a passage that addresses a conquered people. Jerusalem had already fallen and the prophet introduces the radical idea of restoration. First he expresses the despair of the people: "But Zion said, 'The Lord has forsaken me, and my Lord has forgotten me.'"

Then Isaiah comforts them and speaks of restoration with God's words that say *He* has not forsaken or forgotten them:

> *Can a woman forget her nursing child,*
> *And not have compassion on the son of her womb?*
> *Surely they may forget,*
> *Yet I will not forget you.*
> *See I have inscribed you on the palms of my hands;*
> *Your walls are continually before me.* (Isa. 49:15–16)

Can a mother's love fail? The initial answer is "No!" It is contrary to nature. But Isaiah concedes it is possible, though very unlikely. And on that level alone we have enormous comfort. In this metaphor, God's love to his people is *like* that of a mother for her newborn child. This image of a child at its mother's breast and her tender and solicitous, protective care—this should speak to us of God! You say, "The Lord has forgotten!" Consider, can a woman forget her child? Not likely.

But this passage goes much further. It allows for the unthinkable: A mother may forget her own child. This is an admission that speaks to our own desperate age when a young mother has run out of options and her infant is killed or abandoned. Mothers do indeed forget, or worse. But God will not forget. Our names are engraved upon his hands and ever before him. The extremities and social policies which might incite a mother to act against her own child cannot affect the Almighty. He is unchangeably loving, an eternal refuge.

During missionary years in Henderson, Argentina, my parents knew an elderly washerwoman, Doña Maria. When asked, "How many children do you have?" she would smile and shake her head. "I think seventeen," she said. But every so often one would show up and test her memory. Raúl was one of the brood and had misspent his years in alcoholic dissipation on the streets of Buenos Aires. One day he turned up at his mother's door.

"Don't you know me, Señora?" he asked.

She looked him over detachedly with no visible sign of recognition.

"I'm Rául," he said. "Your son."

She inspected more closely and, sure enough, found some signs of identity beneath the grime.

The result was always the same. She took the prodigal in and cleaned him up with her fleshy washerwoman hands. Out of her meager store, she gave her son a fresh start.

All of us need someone we can turn to the way a lost child turns to its mother. There is no posturing or pretension there. There is no great effort to minimize the offense. It is more a matter of casting ourselves upon such people with abandon, trust, humility.

At a recent family reunion that included my sisters and their spouses, we sat around discussing yet another fallen clergyman, a friend of the family who had recently been defrocked over a still shocking moral charge. The misdemeanor had been both sexual and financial and was quite the simmering scandal in the local papers. But this man, whom we had all known fairly well, was not without support. Besides having the denominational support network, he had apparently maintained his innocence so convincingly to those closest to him that they all, especially his sister, stood by him to the end.

"But you can't blame her," said my sister Kathy, who is as good a loyal, true-blue friend as any man could ask. "If it were my brother, I'd believe him."

I said, "Thanks a lot." There is something about family ties.

At a recent conference, Peter Wagner called on ministers to develop circles of support, two or three people who are close enough to you to prayerfully support the deepest areas of your life. He stressed the critical nature of this during times of moral attack. And the point applies to everyone. We all need those we can lean on.

I told a disbelieving crowd of middle class, westernized males that we are "lousy" at sharing. They looked at me with a healthyself look, as well they should. I don't share without trust. I don't share without respect. Too often, I just don't share. But I laid the statistics on my captive audience anyway. "Who are we kidding, guys?" I said. "We are light years behind women when it comes to sharing at a deep level. What you and I call 'intimate conversation,' they call 'small talk.'"

I cited the facts as best I could: Sociologists say that 70 percent of men have many acquaintances, but few close friends, and that we consider that a serious void. This is due largely to our depersonalized society, which is fed by our mobility. Every twenty-four hours more than 100,000 North Americans change residence in pursuit of education, better jobs, different lifestyles. Then there is the ethic of competition which governs a great deal of our work lives. The higher we advance in a company, the greater the stress; the greater the stress, the more we need friends. But the more we need friends, the more difficult it is for us to enjoy them. If you are moving up the corporate ladder and winning by intimidation, by looking out for number one, it is very difficult to adopt the kind of openness that friendship demands. The fact is that at least one person in four now lives alone, or with non-relatives, up 88 percent since 1970.

Despite the obvious need for friendship that such a society generates, we men have difficulty giving each other affection. "He just sat there," said one young man about his closest friend. "I was crying about how my dad had never been affectionate and now he was dead and it was too late. He just sat there and watched me sob, not showing me any love, not touching me—just like my old man!"

Why do we find it so difficult to express affection? What kind of homophobic paranoia has gripped us? Fifty-eight percent of us have not told a best friend that we like him. Many men die without ever knowing how much they mattered to their friends. One man said, "I tend not to admit I love someone, if he is male, until after he can't hear me. That is a cold witness."

Creating a circle of intimate friends who will prayerfully support you will not happen automatically. Somehow we need to make it happen. There is too much at stake to turn away. If we can take the risk of reaching out to one another, we will find a great kind of shelter. Companionship and friendship in this fast-paced world can be one of the most comforting shelters we have.

Beyond such support is that offered by God himself. He is pictured in Isaiah as a mother figure so that his people might run to him with the same kind of complete trust we reserve for our mothers. His kingdom is made up of childlike people who have "converted and become as little children" (Matt. 18:3). This means humility and trust. We demonstrate our childlike humility when we come to the Lord with no concerns about our rags, the appropriateness of our requests, our lostness, our dissipation. We know he cares for us in an unqualified, motherly way. Even when what we share with him will make us look bad, we cast ourselves down at his doorstep and upon his love. We bring reproach on the family and what does he do? He kills the fatted calf for a party with our loved ones!

Chapter 5

Like a Walled Garden

One of my favorite forts was a lush city block in Lomas de Za-
morra, a suburb of Buenos Aires. In the late fifties my father had
purchased the old German estate for a Bible college. It had great
iron gates and a stone wall and was filled with dense foliage: large
fruit trees, vines, ferns, and shrubs. Our house was a converted
gardener's residence at the back, with bright windows and a loft
for me. From the house a windy pathway led through thick, flow-
ering trees to the lawns of the large residence-turned-college at the
center of the property.

During the long summers I climbed thick vines to the balcony
that encircled the building. An iron ladder on the wall led three
stories up to the flat roof where among the turrets I could survey
my entire domain. On a windy day I would fly my kites off the roof
or nestle beside one of the wide water tanks and enjoy my superior
vantage point on the world. I remember chasing about my forested
land like a jungle lord, now scaling trees for a sunny feast of figs
and *nisperos,* now inviting some neighborhood kids in for a fantas-
tic game of "Run Sheep Run" amid the thick vines and ferns, now
parking myself in the dense shade of a mulberry bush and strip-
ping the dark purple fruit. I had an imaginary world in that place
that included Jim Bowie, Tarzan, and the Swiss Family Robin-
son—all the company that a boy of twelve could want.

To Isaiah, Judah was like a walled garden. In the parable of

chapter five, the nation is a vineyard in which the owner has done
everything right. He has planted the "choicest vines" and walled in
his property. But all this care is for nought. This perverse vineyard
has yielded nothing but wild grapes. In disgust, the owner takes
away the hedge, breaks down the wall and says "Let it be trampled." No, the nation is not producing what it should. Rather than
justice, the people produce bloodshed and cries of anguish. Un-
justly, they hoard the best real estate. They indulge in drunken
revelry and are distinguished by a startling lack of insight.

> *They do not pay attention to the deeds of the Lord,*
> *Nor do they consider the work of His hands.*
> *Therefore, My people go into exile for their lack of*
>   *knowledge.* (Isa. 5:12–13 NASV)

They remind us of that ragtag bunch of villains who take over a
vineyard in one of Jesus' parables. They beat up the rent collectors
and finally kill the son and heir. This vineyard, they say, will be
ours. But inevitably the landowner's patience with these men runs
out. Land that should be profitable is not. It is enough to make him
reconsider the investment: "The earth which drinks in the rain that
often comes upon it, and bears herbs useful for those by whom it is
cultivated, receives blessing from God; but if it bears thorns and
briars, it is rejected and it is near to being cursed, whose end is to
be burned" (Heb. 6:7–8).

Judah was planted in its land for better things. The land is des-
tined to be, in Isaiah's terms, "like the garden of the Lord" (Isa.
51:3). In the long run, "The Lord will . . . satisfy your soul in
drought, And strengthen your bones; You shall be like a watered
garden, And like a spring of water, whose waters do not fail" (Isa.
58:11). But in the meantime, this unseemly crop of injustice and
oppression must give way: "As a garden causes the things sown in
it to spring up. So the Lord GOD will cause righteousness and
praise to spring up before all the nations" (Isa. 61:11 NASV). The
nation was behaving as though it had no wall of protection at all. Its
wild grapes could grow any old place. Yet it had been spaded,
cleared of stones, walled, and hedged, and was complete with a

watchtower and a winepress. All of that for wild grapes, bitter and sour.

The owner had put a pile of work into this vineyard. The limestone outcroppings of the typical Judean hillside produced an infinite number of stones. To build a decent vineyard, the rocks had to be hauled out by hand. Usually they could be used to build the surrounding wall, making the most of the resources and impediments. Thorny bushes were planted alongside the wall to deter predators. Only then was the owner ready to plant the vines, and once they were planted, he had a two-year wait before the first harvest. This down time was used for reinforcing the wall, building the tower, and hewing out the winepress. This is when the labor really got intensive. Two vats were hewn out of limestone, one above the other, and connected by a shallow trough. The upper one was used for pressing the grapes; the lower, lined in plaster, was a deeper settling basin for the juice that ran down the trough. Building a vineyard was no small task, and there were no shortcuts. The owner could count on a lot of aches and pains just to get set up.

Isaiah's point with this story is clear: This nation was more privileged than it realized. Even at this tenuous time in its history, it had all the ingredients for national health and prosperity. Its gross crop was inexcusable.

Many of us live in the kind of privileged environment that could be called a "fertile hill." There is much good in the soil. If we forget for a while the greener pastures of our fantasies, we are faced with a great possibility: *the place where we are is very fertile soil*. We can be as productive right here as anywhere else on earth.

Spending too long wishing for greener pastures can keep you from being effective where you are. Put your roots down there. Accept the place of your planting as a special provision. Begin to absorb the resources of fertility that are all around you. As you do, you will find obstacles and impediments being removed. "Putting your roots down" means making the most of your present environment, not living for tomorrow or dreaming of being somewhere else. It means enhancing your present home as though you expect to be there forever. It means developing relationships with people here and now that are built for the long haul. It means discovering the wealth of culture and experience that *your* place has to offer.

How many times have we been visited by an eager tourist and said, "She's seen more of this town in five days than we have in five years!" The resources of our very rich and rewarding terrain were not being cultivated. We mustn't let that happen. I golfed with a semi-retired gentleman last summer who had lived in three or four major cities across the country over the past twenty years in the course of his business: Detroit, Montreal, Denver, now Calgary—he was a typical mobile businessman, but he looked back on Halifax as his "fertile hill." "I was very happy in Halifax," he said. "I just didn't know it until I had left." With fertility all around us all of us are happier than we know. Far too often we discover the richness of our gardens looking back.

The best thing about hanging around with our seniors' group, the "Young at Heart," is that they are committed to the fertility of their environment. Recently we toured the city's Center for the Performing Arts, a stunning combination of four theaters and a symphony hall in the heart of Calgary. We saw the beautiful Edith Cohen Theater, designed in the Italian style, with seating for over 700. Another theater just next door is smaller and more intimate, built horseshoe shape according to Shakespearean tradition. Then we went over to the symphony hall where we heard a noon-hour concert on the beautiful new pipe organ. Lunch followed in the lovely Wheatsheaf Dining Room, which overlooks the new Olympic Plaza and City Hall. We saw it all in three hours! The month before, we traveled out to Bow Falls, a dazzling cataract in the foothills. Whether it's a bus tour to the beautiful Kananaskis Lakes nestled in the Canadian Rockies, a day at Banff, a tour of the Energeum, these people keep their agendas very full just being fully alive where they are!

Inside each of us, there is great potential for fruitfulness and creativity. We are made up of "the choicest vines." We need to think of ourselves that way. A positive and grateful attitude toward yourself helps to keep you productive. It keeps you from a sense of inferiority or marginality. The vineyard of life is filled with people of destiny who have been carefully selected and set apart. For this reason alone, our lives should produce good things. Such a view of ourselves also keeps us from throwing our lives away on drugs, booze, promiscuity, and suicide.

Even at their lowest point, Isaiah's people were chosen people of destiny. In his lovely image of choice vines, he dared them to believe that. Moreover, the image of the walled vineyard speaks of a great investment in shelter that someone has made. It reminds us of ancestors who sacrificed to protect a free society, of parents who provided a secure and nurturing home, of school and work opportunities that enrich our lives. Many of us benefit from the painstaking care of myriads of people.

Isaiah's story points out some reasons why people make the kind of sacrifices they do for shelter. Walls are important for what they keep out. Grazing, trampling, thorns and briars are the stuff that can overrun a life without protection. When a life is left open to everything society offers, it is easy prey. It can be pillaged by destructive spiritual forces.

Walls are also important for what they keep in. Parameters actually make our lives richer. We are protected to be creative. Without shelter, we are hard, bitter, and sour. It is only through training and containment, through discipline, that we flourish. The guest cellist at our symphony demonstrated this truth: her virtuoso performance was the product of twenty years of disciplined daily practice. Couples who testify to the rich intimacy within marriage make the same point. And sprinter Carl Lewis would say the same about his 9.8-second 100-meter sprint. We do our best work within the walls of discipline. For all that, though, ultimately shelter is optional. With all the care that has gone into providing it, and all the benefits of respecting it, we are free to live as though it did not exist at all.

No doubt Isaiah uses the wall to point to God's moral law. Judah was a privileged nation, the inheritors of the Mosaic code, which gave them the most enlightened social and moral formula of their time. Respecting the code and living by it would enrich their society immeasurably. Murder, adultery, theft, and lying would have had no place among them. Even covetousness, which is incipient theft and murder, was walled out by the decalogue. But sadly, these things had overrun the nation and produced a "harvest of bloodshed" and "cries of distress."

What do you say to a nation that is determined to live without moral guidelines, to treat human life as though it were animal life, to live wild and dissipated as though the pleasure of the moment were life's only directive? Probably our message today is the same as Isaiah's: Seek shelter in God's walled garden.

Chapter 6

Like Having a Spouse

I asked my wife, Ruth, if I was like a protector to her. She smiled wide-eyed at me and said, "Of course, darling." The truth is, she protects me as often as I her. She has sheltered me from bankruptcy more than once. And she rushes to my defense when I am maligned. I like the way she, my most penetrating critic, can become my most vocal defender. "You laid it on a little thick, didn't you?" I say, after she has taken a cue in a conversation to extol my virtues. I think she believes this guy who doesn't plead his own cause enough is widely misunderstood. Nor does he pick his issues carefully enough. Her mission is to occasionally clarify—he does not sleep all day; he has ideas.

It leaves me wondering if this is not true of most wives. Give them half a chance and they will rush to their husbands' defenses, no matter how indefensible a man's position may sometimes be.

"It's such a long shot," my friend said over one memorable breakfast. "For me to be restored to the Christian ministry after the way I've lived . . . being such a rat, I just—"

"No, listen," his wife interjected, looking across at me. "I always think he's being much too hard on himself."

Remarkable woman, driven by a God-like love, she looked beyond faults that were glaring and gross enough to shatter most marriages and saw the man's need. Too hard on himself? I knew some good brethren who were advocating the lash. But his wife, the primary victim, called for mercy and restoration.

Your wife can also protect you from yourself. We were just starting to enjoy a little California holiday when Ken, the owner of the vacation spot, and I locked horns over the swirling waters of the jacuzzi.

"Where does he get off, putting up a sign like that?" I asked Ruth. " 'Please replace cover after use.' He's got the only place in town that covers the thing at all! Talk about cheap. I'll tell him, 'Look, just put a little extra on my tab for the heat, okay? Just give me two weeks of uninterrupted, accessible, hot jacuzzi with no hassles. Whaddya say? Is that asking so much?' But he has the nerve to ask *his guests* to do it *for* him! It's outrageous!"

Ruth was reading at the time and did not seem to hear all of my outburst. But I was getting pretty steamed without getting anywhere near the pool. When I did go in, I flung the cursed cover against the fence and stalked out disdainfully when I was done. *That* I would not stoop to. And I heard his howls of protest across the courtyard: "I asked him nicely, too, Betty! I thought I was nice about it! 'We keep ours *covered,*' I said."

There was a principle involved, of course, and I was unmovable. *We* would move even if it meant reloading the car with fourteen bags, but *I* would not follow those outrageous directives.

It took the women to resolve things. Betty, the owner, and Ruth, the wife, went to the flea market next morning while over the top of my book I kept one eye on the poolside clock, waiting for the official unveiling at 10 A.M., the ceremonial opening of the emerald green pool to the masses, duly tested for chemicals, the gate officially unlocked. Why was he always late unlocking?

Later, Ruth told me about the shopping venture and her friend Betty. "She takes such an interest in the place. . . . You know the fruit they serve with the complimentary breakfast? She selects that fresh every day! And yes, the grapefruit are off their own trees! She let me choose the flowers today—come take a look at them."

We ended up having a cool beverage with Betty and Ken under their patio umbrella—and, you guessed it, I spread the jacuzzi cover evenly for two weeks, after every use. We headed home thinking the unthinkable, that the place was quaint and quiet and we might like to return someday.

Without such shelter, I would be like a professor friend who fixates interminably on her issues. There is always a "principle" involved. And no, she will not stoop to those unreasonable demands. My job one year was to help break the hold of the issue on her from time to time. "Yes, there is an 'old boys club' in power here." "Indeed they are ignorant and self-indulgent." "Yes, we must be unflinching in our stand for truth." "But," I ask, "could we not attempt another look at the broad picture?"

My impression is that my friend thinks God has spoken more often than he actually has. She also thinks too readily that the issue is no longer in doubt. Things get set in stone. And unless someone comes along and helps liberate her, she fixates on the perceived injustice forever. The issue flares up at the most unexpected moments, offending most people present, piercing an innocent conversation like a knife, right at the top of a long list of perceived grievances. I helped her all I could that year but the shelter I could provide wasn't enough. Someone needs to take my friend to the flea market.

I shelter my wife too. I sense her need for security as she walks by my side on a strange street in Puerto Vallarta. I come to her defense when she is being chewed out by one of our kids: "Hey, leave your mother alone." I try to keep the house from coming down around her, knowing how important physical shelter and order are to her. I'm her protector. A husband is still that, isn't he? Initiator, leader, ruler, the one who calls forth—the structure of the male body seems to indicate such things. On the other hand, women's bodies are different, as Elisabeth Elliot dared write to her daughter:

Yours is the body of a woman. What does it signify? Is there invisible meaning in its visible signs—the softness, the smoothness, the lighter bone and muscle structure, the breasts, the womb? Are they utterly unrelated to what you yourself are?

Isn't your identity intimately bound up with these material forms? Does the idea of you—Valerie—contain the idea of, let's say, "strapping" or "husky?" How can we bypass matter in our search for understanding the personality?[1]

The New Testament concept of headship carries a similar message concerning the husband's role as his wife's protector and head of the family. Headship is like shelter: "The husband is the head of the wife, even as Christ is the head of the church and is the savior of the body" (Eph. 5:23). In this, his highest view of marriage, Paul uses the Greek word *kephale* to indicate the husband's role in marriage. The word was used in Paul's day to indicate the top of a pillar. It was also used for the mouth of a river or the prow of a ship. Paul uses it to point to our Lord and his caring and completing servanthood. A husband should aspire to that, he says, to emulate Christ's care of the church. To be the head is to infuse a relationship with fresh life, like the mouth of a river, to absorb the buffeting of stormy weather on behalf of a family, leading the way through uncharted seas.

We were too busy catching lake trout on carefully tied smelt to notice the squall. The day was still bright over Lake Minnewanka, in the heart of the Rockies. But the wind had picked up and by the time we looked back toward the boat ramp, we were looking at whitecaps. Four-foot waves covered the lake, and we hadn't even reached the bend in the dog-leg. The black cliffs of shale around the lake gave an ominous backdrop to the scene.

What had been a five-minute trip in the little fishing boat going out, turned into a two-hour battering coming back. Crashing through the towering waves left us all drenched and blue-lipped in the icy mountain waters. Four boys screamed with delight as we crashed along from one breaker to the next, but their fathers worried. The prow had to stand the test. Somehow it broke those waves most every time, deflecting the icy waters off to the sides. Occasionally it would meet an extra large wave that would break right over the bow and give everyone a good soaking. But mostly we just got the spray.

The prow of that little fishing boat is a symbol of headship. To lead the way through life's adventures, to crash through the storms that would threaten a family's well-being, to show courage in the face of the most daunting foes, that is what it means to be a husband, the head of the family. At its best, headship guarantees the passengers delight and enjoyment. It opens the door to adventure because it is not afraid to risk. It deflects blows, as much as possible, for the good of the family.

Married love is the most sheltering kind of love. The "Nova Shalom" course we share with couples describes sex as "the most profound means of relaxation available to you." There is something about it within the marriage covenant that is shelter in the fullest sense. There is the sense of being covered, of being enveloped in each other, of being buried—all the ingredients of the best fortress are there in a marriage. It's little wonder the lover is described in fortress terms in the best love songs. There is, of course, the "hold me" theme which calls for "the right to hold you ever so tight," in every generation. And what a sense of refuge one feels in Solomon's love song:

> *Your neck is like the tower of David*
> *Built with rows of stones,*
> *On which are hung a thousand shields,*
> *All the round shields of the mighty men.* (Song 4:4 NASV)

> *"You are as beautiful as Tirzah, my darling,*
> *As lovely as Jerusalem,*
> *As awesome as an army with banners."* (Song 6:4 NASV)

"Cover me," says Ruth at the foot of Boaz' bed. "Spread the corner of your garment over me" (Ruth 3:9 NIV). The man starts thinking of marriage right away.

The pain of divorce has much to do with the loss of shelter. The tears of children and a deserted wife are often matched later by the agony of a disillusioned man who finds himself strangely exposed in the very lifestyle that he thought would be ideal.

My friend, I'll call him Gary, would like nothing better right now than to rebuild his shattered home. He sheds the tears that most of us would do anything to avoid—tears for a loving home that he destroyed two years ago. I remember the pastoral moments with his wife. "Do you know, Pastor?" she said. "That man put his arms around me right there in the restaurant and started to cry. He sobbed and sobbed."

It was Gary's last stand. As I understand it, he had been seduced by a woman he worked with. But he was still connected to his family, two teen-agers and a wife. "Mid-life struggle," we all said. He was like a wounded bird struggling to regain its flight. But the arrow had plunged deep.

He severed the ties. None of his friends could believe it. He moved to California with his new-found love. The rest of us tried to pick up the pieces. I remember quoting Daniel Levinson's *Seasons of a Man's Life* to Gary's son trying to explain "mid-life." I felt like I understood it a bit; Gary and I were both in our early forties. "At this age," I said, "men have to rearrange the furniture of their lives. Something must change. Either you change spouse, job, home, and career, or you change your approach to those things. Change is critical in mid-life."

I knew very well the sense of entrapment that descends on a man and the desperation to do *something* before it's too late. That sudden awareness of mortality changes a man's outlook on everything. It really has nothing to do with whether or not you love your wife. It is the sense of entrapment that makes you feel you have to break away somehow before it is too late, and you end up having lived your life for nothing.

Fortunately, we *can* make the right changes. We can use time differently and build relationships with people we might previously have ignored. Mentoring can become something we enjoy. We can pass on something of ourselves to a new generation. The old compulsions about upward mobility tend to lose their force. If you make the *right* changes, you can emerge around age forty-five a much more mellow and together person.

But Gary is far from "together" today. His changes were far too drastic for his own good, never mind what they did to his wife and kids. He tore down the shelter of home and can't find the means now, two years later, to rebuild it. And, for what did he do it? For emptiness? For the vanity of the dry-waller's life he now leads? For his latest live-in? I'm sure every time he applies the joint-filler, it is a message about reinforcing the relationships of life, of bonding. Gary is the closest I have come to observing the deliberate destruction of shelter. It is not pretty. Better the most modest fortress than that.

We like to spend some summer days at a cottage with my seventy-year-old parents-in-law. The original bunkie they bought back in the sixties on Beaver Lake has been surpassed now with a large chalet, so they can host their four kids and their families once a year, if possible. The last family to arrive gets the bunkie. What great moments we have, spreading two picnic tables on the wide deck with tacos, burgers, and fish hot off the fire after a long day on the water.

My father-in-law presides over the festivities with all the dignity of a lord of the manor. He is enjoying the benefits of some fifty years of faithfulness to a spouse and family. Surrounded by his affectionate children, watching the emerging personalities of his ten grandchildren, the man has a wealth about his life that money could never buy.

What is it about the glue that has held his marriage and family together? Is there a formula that we could bottle and sell? Can he pass it on to the rest of us? Did this couple navigate the mid-life years because there was less of an assault on fidelity then than we experience now?

A family of raccoons took over the deck at a recent reunion, waddling down to the water from the dark woods, their soft little padded feet carrying fat, furry bodies. We discourage the grandchildren from feeding these masked bandits. Once they get food, they stake a claim on a place and take over. But one night we bent the rules a bit for the sake of the younger children who hadn't seen raccoons that close up. The mother ate right out of my five-year-old niece's trembling hand. The cubs watched warily, still too spooked for human contact. With one loud simulated bark from one of us, they darted up a tree, never to reappear. The father snapped and snarled ferociously over a bees' nest he discovered in a tree stump. He would brook no interference from one of his older sons. When the excitement was over, the family vanished into the night. But they would be back for sure. The thought of Cheerios and honey would warrant many a return visit.

The human family will also continue to return. Our families are held together by something in the natural order that is much stronger than the moral darkness of the times or the barks of the prophets of doom who predict their demise. Add to the natural order the strength of a marriage covenant and the accompanying blessing of God and you have a very strong bond. The family may seem to vanish into the night of our times. But nourished by a strong faith, a family unity can withstand the rigors of life over fifty years.

Part 3

Shelter Is a Secret Place

African nights. For a good dark night you can't beat Africa. It's quite unlike my neighborhood where we are overrun with beastly streetlights. It is almost like around the clock daylight. You would think that the city fathers would understand that if we wanted twenty-four-hour daylight we could live in one of those northern towns like Inuvik where during half the year the sun never sets. I enjoy the sunrise, and I also love sunset. And after the sun goes down, I like to feel, in Hopkins' words, "the fell of dark, not day."

Once I was so frustrated with a great looming light leaning over our back fence, I took an extension ladder and scaled the thing. All around the side that shone into our yard I painted its leering orange face with a coat of black paint. Now it serves its purpose perfectly. It casts a soft light on the pedestrians below who jog along the green belt out back, and leaves our yard in the dark. Mind you the best solution would be to shorten it so it could function more like the streetlights in Palm Springs where they are attached to the border palms and never higher than knee level or so. There the spell of night is allowed to dominate. Perhaps I should have used a saw instead of a paintbrush.

We sat by a fire within the walled campus of Pan African Christian College listening to the BBC crackle its short wave news report. Soviet minister Shevardnaze was meeting U.S. Secretary of State George Shultz at a summit meeting on disarmament in Switzerland. "That all seems so far removed from us now," my host said.

As the vast dark stillness settled around us, I knew what he meant. "Back in Vancouver, we were vitally interested in what happened at such summits," he said. "There with all the submarine bases nearby, you are a potential target in a nuclear strike. But out here . . ."

We were covered by a vast canopy of dark. Oh there were some risks. There were black mamba snakes underfoot, and there was the continuing threat of vandalism. But the dominant sense for me was peaceful shelter. It was a sense I seemed to recognize: of having disappeared from life as we know it, of being erased and swallowed up in the vast darkness—kind of buried. Yes, I felt buried in the African night. Not buried in death, but in a new kind of subterranean life.

If there had been caves around my childhood homes, I'm sure I would have been in them often. The rooting around in the snow that I did do, the burrowing and scraping like a rodent, was a big part of my childhood. I remember burrowing, burrowing in a big double bed at night until I was all scrunched around the bottom, buried in the suffocating warmth of blankets while my sister poked around trying to find me, and then bursting out gasping for fresh air.

Similarly, there were the underwater games we played during the summer. They were always accompanied by the sense of being buried and the wish that we could stay under there as a new antediluvian form of deep sea life. If we were transformed into giant creatures of the deep, we could skim along the sandy bottom of then clean Lake Ontario, touching the ribboned sand. Out of sight, and feeling transformed, we would cruise from the shadow of one submerged boulder to the next.

This idea of immersion, of being lost and found in a more intimate, secret state is part of some great shelters. To be lost in distance, for example, in a lovely quiet villa, separated by two thousand miles or so from mundane concerns is the essence of a

truly restorative holiday. The distance is not great enough, however, if all you do is case business deals in another part of the
world. The distance is not great enough if the villa is close to home
and you have your portable phone along to keep in contact.

We were in Palm Springs. It was a most breathtakingly beautiful
March morning. Surrounded by the most spectacular view of the
Sierra Mountains, we watched a young businessman wallow in the
jacuzzi like a great walrus while talking business on his portable
phone. He was doing it all wrong. He had brought his everyday
concerns to his restorative shelter and consequently had destroyed
it.

The combination of distance and quiet can be truly restorative.
Even a brief vacation when you are immersed in distance and quiet
can accomplish more inner restoration than a longer, more harried
one.

Darkness and distance are not the only things that can bury us.
Our first home as a married couple was on the subterranean level
of the building that housed our first church. Every winter our
home was buried literally by huge drifts of snow that blew in at
night. There was nothing on the outskirts of Montreal to impede
the thick white blanket that swept in from the north, and we would
wake up next day to find ourselves submerged. I visit my friendly
chiropractor to this day because of my ill-advised frontal attack on
the six-foot drifts I had to plough through just to get to the car,
which was also buried.

What a way to go, though, if you are going to be buried. There
is something about all that white, sifting silence, the way the snow
drifts in around you, that makes it an attractive form of entomb-
ment. Like the water games of my childhood and the comfortable
canopy of the African darkness, the sheltered feeling that comes
after a snowfall is most peaceful.

In one of my father's poems, snow is a soft, enchanting symbol
of divine grace. He calls the poem "Soft Falls the Snow."

> Soft falls the snow
> A jeweled veil of costly lace;
> Each flake unique,
> Patterned by hand divine

And scattered from his fingers
Like virgin blossoms falling
On the wind
In bounteous measure,
All earth's torn fields
Concealing.
And on this costly treasure
Tramples the foot of man,
Thoughtlessly.

But from His hand of grace,
Like treasured curtain of the snows
Carved from Redemption's plan, there falls
Eternal life for earth-bound souls.
Freely He shed abroad
In bounteous measure
Love's patterned flakes!
Giving his Son, His well-beloved
Even to earth, and cross and tomb,
Redeeming!
And on this costly treasure
Hast thou trampled
Foot of man?[1]

We buried Sophia Brown out in Banff's mountain cemetery. There had been a heavy snowfall the night before so that our little graveside gathering was in the midst of the most spellbinding winter wonderland I had ever seen. The gravestones were like lumps on a thick layer of whipped cream. The boughs of the evergreens that towered all around us sagged beneath the clumped-on weight of a foot of snow. The sun broke through the puffy clouds and diamonds seemed to sparkle on the fresh layer of white. It was the Christmas season. I spoke to the dear folk about the greatest gift— God's covering of righteousness for all our sin. It is a permanent, majestic blanket. "Calvary covers it all," we sang, "my past with its sin and shame."

Distance and darkness, water and snow, all kinds of things go into this sense of burial that has made up some of my best shelters.

These are elements that I continue to seek in my favorite retreats. Essentially, however, there must be secrecy. To be totally immersed, lost and then found in a more intimate state, the shelter must be inaccessible, a secret hiding place that is unknown to the world. It must be exempt from all demands, a place where the humdrum concerns of ordinary mortals cannot invade and you cannot intervene in the larger concerns of the world even if you want to. It must allow you to be free to have a rich inner life and, at the same time, to explore the depths of the lake or pool, or to talk in hushed tones with friends by a fire.

Ah, the shelter of a secret place.

Chapter 7

Your Sealed Room

It was a long, hot summer, a Buenos Aires summer. The humid lush days stretch out in my memory as infinite. I climbed the colonnade encircling the stone building that was my castle, leaping from vine-covered trellis to trellis, over the two-foot spaces in between, some twenty feet above the ground. And as I traversed the side of the building, I tested the shutters.

This place was shut up tighter than Jericho and I wanted access. Tap, tap, push, pull—there has to be an opening for a stealthy intruder, I thought. Finally a shutter gave and I looked through window-panes into a dormitory bedroom. I opened the window and stole through into the interior darkness, a bold intruder in broad daylight penetrating the hushed interior of the institution in the heat of summer. I pulled the shutter closed behind me.

How long I stayed I do not recall. But one blazing summer afternoon was wiled away in a cool dark retreat. Unobserved, I peeked through the lattices. It was wonderful.

During the 1990 Persian Gulf crisis there must have been more sealed rooms than dining rooms in Tel Aviv and Jerusalem. The people need sealed rooms when missiles are falling, so the experts say, especially if they are carrying chemicals. In the same threatened land, but in another time, Isaiah called his people to hide inside:

> *Come, my people, enter your chambers,*
> *And shut your doors behind you;*

> *Hide yourself as it were, for a little moment,*
> *Until the indignation is past.* (Isa. 26:20)

Scorching sun, outpoured indignation, Scud missiles, all call for a room in which to hide.

The indignation talked about in Isaiah is God's wrath. It will be poured out on the earth, but God's people will be spared. "The Lord is about to come out of his place to punish the inhabitants of the earth for their iniquity" (Isa. 26:21). This warning reminds us of the horsemen of the Apocalypse and the judgments associated with history's climax when seven seals will be broken and dreadful judgments sent forth on the earth. One of the four horsemen will sit on a red horse and take peace from the earth "that men should slay one another" (Rev. 6:4). One will bring famine, and another will cause one quarter of the earth's population to die. There will be earthquakes and catalysmic upheavals. Everyone will seek shelter. "The kings of the earth and the great men and the commanders and the rich and the strong and every slave and free man, hid themselves in the caves and among the rocks of the mountains; and they said to the mountains and to the rocks, 'Fall on us and hide us from the presence of Him who sits on the throne, and from the wrath of the Lamb; for the great day of their wrath has come; and who is able to stand?'" (Rev. 6:15–17).

What visions of dreadful judgment! No wonder people scurry for shelter. But shelter won't be provided for the masses. It will be denied to all but the chosen. An old spiritual grasps the urgency of this final rush for shelter:

> Oh my lovin' brother, when the world's on fire,
> Don't you want God's bosom for to be your pillow?
> Hide me over in the Rock of Ages,
> Rock of ages cleft for me.

> Down here, down here, there's no hidin' place down here.
> Oh I went to the rock to hide my face, the rock cried out,
> "No hidin' place!
> No hidin' place down here."

Prophecy students like to remind us that there will always be a shelter for God's people. God never pours out judgments without sheltering his people first. Noah's ark and the rushed exit of Lot and family from Sodom indicate the pattern. Fire and brimstone will not fall until the righteous are removed. Hence the teaching of the rapture of the church. Before the seals are broken at the end of time, it is argued, the church of Christ will be caught away to a sheltered place, "and so shall we ever be with the Lord." This "taking out," it is maintained, is none other than the removal of the church so that the Anti-Christ can carry out his program of mass-destruction unimpeded: "He who now restrains will do so until He is taken out of the way" (2 Thess. 2:7). The place of shelter, then, would be a distant place, a removed place, a place with the Lord.

We hear the call of Isaiah in a similar vein: "Come, my people . . . hide for a little while." This is an invitation. It is a calling away. And it may well be the most critical invitation ever extended.

Lasting shelter during times of indignation—we should run for that.

Chapter 8

In Another Sealed Room

And when you pray, you shall not be like the hypocrites. For they love to pray standing in the synagogues and on the corners of the street that they may be seen by men. Assuredly I say to you they have received their reward. But when you pray, go into your room, and when you have shut your door, pray to your Father who is in the secret place; and your Father who sees in secret, will reward you. (Matt. 6:5–6)

This is a call to a private devotional life that is quite removed from the public clamor and display often associated with piety.

In the ancient world, very pious Jews took pains to demonstrate their piety publicly. That caused them to miss the whole concept of prayer as shelter. They prayed loudly on street corners. Apparently the impression made on passers-by was greater than it would be today, for we might wonder who left the gates to certain institutions open. But back then people were impressed. "They have their reward," says our Lord.

In our day as well, much that passes for piety is for public show. We march, we protest, we boycott and shout. Our great gatherings are televised and often attract thousands of people. But much of our display is sheer hypocrisy. It really has nothing to do with prayer, the secret matter: "Pray to your Father who is in secret and your Father who sees in secret will reward you." Our Lord seems to echo the Old Testament invitation to enter your room and hide for a little while.

I think this is the most attractive aspect of prayer. It combines the isolation and sense of removal we would find in a fort with the strength and nurture of companionship. And it demonstrates a great paradox of faith: The most happens when nothing is happening, or we exercise our greatest strength when we fold our hands in prayer.

In the parable of the "Importunate Widow," Helmut Thielicke sees the strength we find in our helplessness:

> A widow is often a negligible quantity, a non-entity that can be brushed aside.
>
> Are we to believe then that this church, which is represented as a defenseless widow without manly protection, that this church which folds its hands in prayer as a sign of its defenselessness, that this church by its intercession before the throne of God actually shares in the government of the world and participates in the divine ordering of war and peace and curse and blessing? Is not this simply too fantastic to believe? But nothing less than this we are assured and promised.[1]

I discovered the joys of prayer early. I must have been all of ten when I gathered with my summer friends in Cobourg's Children's Tabernacle for Kids Camp meetings. Patched knees in the sawdust, faces down on the old wooden benches which were duly carved by all kinds of fancy jack-knives, we prayed for God's mercy. We received the Savior there, a roomful of youngsters, savoring a pocket of light on a cool dark summer night on the north shore of Lake Ontario. My brightest memory is of walking out of that tabernacle one night, knowing that the world was forever changed. It was my spiritual awakening. I discovered the life-changing rewards of prayer there, under a suddenly dazzling summer night's sky.

If my prayer life were to end today, I would desperately miss the shelter. That overpowering sense of being covered is simply indispensable to me. Without it, I feel uneasy about any major decision.

A friend cited the statistics about this continent's ministers: On average, we spend some fifteen minutes a day in prayer. "And you all feel guilty about it," he said.

"Well, we should," I replied.

"Yes," he said, "but think of this. You are on the frontlines of battle. You are the Joshuas of the church. You fight; others pray. The battle is won."

It sounded nice in theory. But I had to tell him that I abandon the fight if I don't pray. I can't make the most basic decisions of church life without a consistent prayer life. There is no frontline for me without my private room. I postpone major decisions until prayer is back to center. Confidence is connected, for me, to being overshadowed by God in prayer. Leadership is dependent upon that. And, at times, I can present the most radical ideas and even carry some of them out with a certain amount of risk when I have that sense. There is how I know I am more than a conqueror.

Without the shelter of prayer, I have little to say. But when my secret place is intact, I can communicate ideas forcefully, with a conviction that is not my own. I spoke a few weeks ago on the importance of "consultation," of not making decisions just on my own because the theme of a decision I needed to make had emerged in prayer. Even though the idea was flown in, so to speak, in the midst of another series and had no direct relation to anything happening in the church at the time, it proved to be most timely and helpful to several people. One couple said, "We're going back to our marriage counselor. We've been trying to resolve everything on our own." It was exactly the right, timely word.

Without the shelter of prayer, I just don't feel right. But when I have it, I feel strong and purposeful. This kind of prayer allows you to center, to focus, on your essential mission. You feel approved. You feel coordinated. You feel that your day will not be wasted, fragmented, misspent. When I have lost that encounter for a time, I know instinctively that my effectiveness is impaired. No amount of additional work will help. The only help is shutting the door and absorbing the blessings of the secret place.

This prayer is silent. Or it may be accompanied with what Paul calls "groanings which cannot be uttered." To me it is most connected with waiting and a form of blank-minded meditation. Kneeling is most helpful for this form of prayer. The body language itself is a statement of helplessness, of intensity of focus. Nobody is going anywhere. The door has been shut. The secret place is everything. This is the moment of encounter. Sometimes my elbows get numb and I change from kneeling at a chair to getting my forehead down on the floor mosque style. There is something about the abject humility of this that is very good for prayer.

And this, to me, is prayer at its strongest. An hour or two of that kind of abject silence is almost a denial of one's own resourcefulness—and yet it can be most strengthening. It is strange that when so little seems to be happening, so much has happened. An outside observer might well conclude that the struggle against sleep has been lost. And, I confess, it has been lost on occasion. But more often there is a growing sense of God's presence in the silence of waiting. The secret place produces the most complete sense of shelter imaginable.

Perhaps this is the "waiting" which is so often stressed in the scriptures. "Those who wait upon the Lord shall renew their strength" (Isa. 40:31). "Wait on the Lord! Be of good courage and he shall strengthen your heart; wait, I say, on the Lord" (Ps. 27:14). Waiting is an expression of helplessness. "As the eyes of a maid [look] to the hand of her mistress, so our eyes look to the Lord our God" (Ps. 123:2). Banished are the wordy petitions which fill other prayer times. No long list of scriptures that might be the content of some very profitable prayer times belongs here. This secret place is governed by silence. Even the anthems of praise that comprise special celebratory times of prayer and praise are not forced into this silent cell.

Sometimes you rise from such a time feeling that no good has come of it. That, of course, is not true and should not be used as a reason for not returning to your private place. My experience is that such a feeling may precede a day of special blessing when the secret place is going to crown your life with the glory of God. The day you don't feel like going is sure to be a day not to miss. So feeling that the time has been unproductive may be your cue to get back to your secret place as quickly as you can.

God's strength is cumulative, I think. A pattern of finding the secret place, a consistent habit of being there, brings a growing sense of divine strength to you. Sometimes, of course, it may be that your prayer time lacks content and you are not being specific enough with your petitions. I find waiting in prayer has to be mixed with more vocal forms of prayer at other times. But this secret place of quiet rest is pure shelter.

I have a couple of very private secret places where I can lock the doors and I am lost to the world. One is a little room in the church which was designed as a changing room for baptismals and is now an unused music room. I have a collapsible chair in there and I enter and disappear. Another is a shed-study I have outside my home. But one of my "secret" places is right out in public view.

I like to take a small stack of business cards on a jog. It's not that I want to distribute them to passers-by; they have prayer requests and dated answers written out on the back. I can tuck them up the sleeve of a windbreaker and, as long as the run lasts, I can read them and pray about them as I do my "rounds." Walking, like jogging, releases the energy I need to *see* some prayers answered. I like that form of prayer.

Praying the scriptures is a great way to keep prayer from becoming a vacuum. I carry my scripture notes in a little three-ring binder. Often it lies open on the seat of the car. Turning a passage into a personal prayer is a marvelous way of revitalizing prayer. We transcend the smallness of our issues when we pray with Paul's great heart. The Psalms enable us to grasp God's greatness. Today my reading was "The Lord visited Sarah as he had said, and did unto her as he had spoken" (Gen. 21:1). And my prayer was: "Lord, *do* unto me as you have said. Fulfill your promises. And act on behalf of Tim and Joan who want a child. Lord, you did this work for Sarah. I confess my complete dependence on you. I need you to do what you alone can do."

The best protestion of your silent time is claiming an early hour of the day. That is when I have my most meaningful moments.

Sometimes the sun rises outside as the presence of the Lord settles inside. And I go from my place ready to tackle the world.

A friend of mine describes his prayer time as, "Then I get this galloping going on the inside." It is the Spirit, he says, confirming that a decision and direction is right. Out of the stillness and silence of private prayer comes a stirring, and sometimes it catapults you onto your feet and into action. I like to resist it as much as possible, because we are all frenetic enough as it is and will grasp any excuse to keep from being still. But more than once I have broken away from prayer on the run, racing away to implement an idea, make a call, record a thought. The transformation has occurred. Strength has been renewed. You enter the quiet place tired, bereft of ideas, strung out; you leave on the run.

My father described the renewal in another of his poems.

> Forth from Thy presence
> With that inner grace
> That glows from heart and face
> In radiant essence.
>
> Forth where spirits languish,
> Where sad hands grope
> For love and light—where hope
> Lies panting in a world's anguish.
>
> Forth from Thy presence, soul aglow
> With the rare loveliness Thou dost bestow.
> With grace o'erflowing, and tend'rest balm
> For a world's sores; each word a psalm.
>
> Our weakness lost
> In matchless strength divine,
> Where task and toil and victory
> Are Thine.[2]

Praise is vital to a prayer life. Some of my best prayer arises at the piano, following a sequence of worship choruses. And sometimes the church sanctuary becomes my prayer room. I can walk about the aisles and raise my voice in prayer. This can be as sheltering as my silent cell. Praise brings God so near—he does indeed "inhabit" praise. And lifting up his name in celebratory vocal praise is a great secret to effective prayer.

Just as when we praise God and he comes near, we also need to draw near to those around us with praise for them. "These inmates need praise," the Warden said, and I knew he was right. He told of one juvenile offender who had done a drafting assignment very well. "You did a superb job on that, Carl," he told the lad. And he told us, "Well, you could just feel the kid grow two feet right there before your eyes! Probably never had a word of praise in his life."

I recalled a relay race in my high school days. My team, Corinth, had lost by a hair to the competition, Athens.

"I thought we had it won!" I lamented to my father after the race. "Did you see the guys we had? We had Gough, we had MacFarlane . . ."

My dad said, "If they had all run as well as you, you *would* have won." And I grew two feet. I can still hear the words.

So I try to hug my kids, with both verbal and physical hugs as often as opportunity and wisdom allow. I know I am far from perfect on this matter of fatherly commendation, but how great to know there is a Heavenly Father whose commendation is always there, whose eye and hug envelop us in continual expressed affection. We grow under his loving eye.

I believe we can project from ourselves to God because we are made in his image. We have this wonderful capacity for affection, and it brings out the absolute best in us, whether we give it or receive it. We bloom in the eyes of love. Can we not assume—must we not insist—that God reaches out to our lives with something similar? That he recognizes our worth, that he compliments our virtues, that he praises our attainments and our efforts and rests his eye upon us with the rapt look of a lover or proud father, that he strokes and caresses and cherishes our lives—all this I believe.

Moreover, God must caress our lives in greater ways, immeasurably greater ways. Our experiences give us an inkling of how vital expressed affection is to life. But our Lord is the very source of love. "Herein is love, not that we loved God, but that he loved us and sent his Son as an atoning sacrifice for our sins. . . . Beloved, let us love one another, for love comes from God" (1 John 4:10–11). It follows that if we, imperfect as we are, know how to express affection to the creatures around us, He must be much more proficient at it. Indeed, this is the very assurance of Jesus' words: "If you, then, being evil, know how to give good gifts to your children, how much more will your heavenly Father give the Holy Spirit to those that ask Him?" (Luke 11:13). How much more? That is the question.

Not only is he the very source of love, but God is the master of expression. The one who shows his love in action, who spoke the worlds into order—how could he possibly be deficient in this matter of expressed affection, like some of the bottled-up males you meet who have the worst possible time saying "I love you" to those they love most?

No, as the source of both love and expression, God leaves us far behind when it comes to letting love show. His divine caress is around us continually, and prayer is our chief means of discovering God's intimate messages of love. We feel his touch when we pray.

Without prayer, I feel unloved. Oh, I am assured by my spouse and friends that I am not unloved; but the divine caress of sheltering prayer, this I prize most of all.

Chapter 9

Covered by an Ocean
of Knowledge

Some of my favorite forts are libraries. Emmanuel College library at the University of Toronto is one of them. It has a very high ceiling and stained glass windows. And I have fond memories of a subterranean cubicle at Queens where I finished preparation for my M.A. comprehensive exam. A flight of stairs wound down into a fairly dark room lighted only by the desk lamps in the cubicles. It was a wonderful little refuge for me surrounded with the learning of the ages.

Perhaps mental furniture that reminds me of classrooms has as much to do with this sense of shelter as anything. There is nothing like an ocean of knowledge to make you feel sheltered. Think about that profound sense of security you get from learning. I appreciate the sense of what I know. This is a great shelter.

I remember my startled awareness when, as a Ph.D. teaching assistant, I discovered that my knowledge of English literature was an ocean compared to that of my freshman students. Then, recently, I sat in Professor Janus Svilpis' class on satire and sensed the incredible range of his familiarity with the subject. How comfortable that seminar was: a little disengaged cluster of academics sharing insights on satire from Swift to Dickens. Name a work and Svilpis could expound on it in some detail. And his thorough grasp, his complete delight in the material, was not unlike the delight of a boy in his fort. "Come, explore with me!" he seemed to say. We hated to disband for the day.

People like this, who absolutely know their subject, influence me most. It is not the volume of the speaker's voice but the volume of his or her learning that I find most compelling. When they deluge me with their ocean of learning, I acquiesce. I am putty in their hands.

One of the most secure feelings you can have comes from knowing all there is to know about your subject. Learning John Donne's canon, scurrilous and sacred, and being able to expound on all of his poems is one of my fondest memories from academia. I remember putting down my well used pen at the end of examination day, knowing that there was nothing more to be said. Strangely enough a little volume I picked up at a bus depot enabled me to know Donne so thoroughly. It is Jerry West's *The Memory Book*. I remember the excitement of that bus trip, not for the scenery, but for the experience of memorizing the States of the Union in about ten minutes. I sensed I had entered a world of incredible potential, where the power of memory could be used to the maximum. Sure enough, that system of memory with images has served me very well ever since, for everything from John Donne's corpus to phone numbers.

Security in your field is a fortress from which you can venture out on information seeking tours. You have a foundation on which to build. James Michener says that an arts major has the skills to understand almost anything. He has learned how to think, and will always be in demand.

"I'm enough of a Baptist," Michener says, "to believe in total immersion." He does not write until he has thoroughly immersed himself in the subject of his choice. Some five years of research create the very credible backlog of information that provides the setting for each of his voluminous novels. "When the ocean is full," he says, "the novel begins to write itself."

I feel that picking up an old book is like re-entering a circle of old friends. When my world gets too trite, I seek out the charmed world of Anthony Trollope and let his Warden resist the fulminating Victorian Archdeacon, who happens to be his son-in-law. Trollope's Warden, in the novel of the same name, is such a Christ-like character, I feel comfortable enough with him to sit by his fire and listen quite often.

In a sense you are untouchable in this secret place. And it is one of the most immediate and enchanted, most inexpensive shelters available to us. "Read Tolkien," said C. S. Lewis. "He is the great therapy after too many daily newspapers." I did. I picked him up after an unpleasant introduction to a lady with red hair, whose spirit was as grating and sour as the worst daily. I wished that I could free her from the gnarling anger that twisted her face. But the best I could do that day, as far as I knew, was to turn to the wonderful world of Tom Bombadil in *Lord of the Rings* and let him burst upon my day with all of his song and sunshine.

I join Allan Bloom in bemoaning the loss of familiarity with great books in contemporary education. He questions his earlier conviction that the human desire to know is universal and permanent, and that all educators really need to do is put the feast on the table. Now he fears a spiritual entropy has taken hold. Futuristic trends have produced education that is little more than propaganda:

> Without the great revelations, epics and philosophies as part of our natural vision, there is nothing to see out there and little left inside. . . . Today's select students know so much less, are so much more cut off from the tradition, are so much slacker intellectually, that they make their predecessors look like prodigies of culture. The soil is ever thinner, and I doubt whether it can now sustain the taller growths.[1]

Bloom's pessimism for the state of knowledge is something Isaiah might have felt for his own people. He saw people who engaged in substance abuse and were condemned to ignorance and ultimate exposure as a result:

> *That they may follow intoxicating drink;*
> *Who continue until night, till wine inflames them! . . .*

> *But they do not regard the work of the LORD,*
> *Nor consider the operation of His hands.*
> *Therefore my people have gone into captivity,*
> *Because they have no knowledge;*
> *Their honorable men are famished.* (Isa. 5:11–13)

In my experience, students who have had a serious fling with drugs—and gotten over it—find it difficult to have enthusiasms or great expectations. It is as though the color has been drained out of their lives and they see everything in black and white. . . . Their energy has been sapped, and they do not expect their life's activity to produce anything but a living.[2]

Spiritual darkness is bound to follow such perverse tastes, say the prophets. Isaiah called his people away from their fascination with the occult and back to their ancient literature. "Should they seek the dead on behalf of the living?" he wondered. No, "to the law and to the testimony! If they do not speak according to this word, it is because there is no light in them" (Isa. 8:19–20). Isaiah knew that knowledge and learning offer the ultimate shelter in times of stress. Only truth provides refuge. He said that the refuge of lies and self-deception will be swept away (see Isa. 28:17). There is a kind of judgment in willful ignorance that makes it impossible to grasp truth:

It seems substance abuse and ignorance went together. And together they produced the exposure of exile and starvation.

In our day, a similar note is sounded by such educators as Allan Bloom:

> *For the LORD has poured out on you*
> *The spirit of deep sleep,*
> *And has closed your eyes, namely, the prophets;*
> *And He has covered your heads, namely, the seers.*

> *The whole vision has become to you like the words of a book*
> *that is sealed.* (Isa. 29:10–11)

There are rebels who reject learning. A fool who speaks nonsense is called noble by the standards of the day; a rogue is called generous (see Isa. 32:5).

For all that, though, Isaiah sounds a hopeful note. Despite the intellectual darkness which surrounded him, he had a bright future vision. On his terms, the ideal society is filled with knowledge. It will come flooding in like a veritable ocean and the "earth shall be full of the knowledge of the Lord" (Isa. 11:9). Isaiah saw a world covered, buried in an ocean of knowledge. And he saw that in the future, of all places.

Imagine such a world. It will be ruled by a prince who has the "spirit of wisdom and understanding, counsel, power, the spirit of knowledge and the fear of the Lord" (Isa. 11:2). His insight will be such that no injustice will take place in his reign, to the needy or the poor. Oppressors will be judged by him. The whole world will be at peace. No creature will harm nor destroy (see Isa. 11:1–8). This is the ideal world that men have always been fascinated with. The ancient prophets said that it would come in the reign of the Messiah. We can still anticipate it today. And we can prepare for it.

This ideal world will be governed by knowledge. We can hasten its arrival by being people of knowledge ourselves. This means resisting anti-intellectualism in all its forms. Sometimes it wears the garb of piety and gives the impression that the more ignorant you are, the more opportunity you give God to perform wonders through you. Surely we are called to offer to God our best.

We can inculcate in children a love for books and seek to wean them from TV early. Preparing for the future also means investing in education. George Barna, in his futuristic *Frog and the Kettle*, anticipates that excellent education will be out of reach for many by the year 2000 and that the church will be called upon to help fill the gap.

We can also fight the scourge of illiteracy in the world. The privilege of reading and writing is not widely and evenly shared across our world. My friend Uwe Gustaffson, who teaches literacy with Wycliffe to the Adavasi tribe of northern India, tells me that a person's sense of worth is closely tied to his ability to read in his native language.

Preparing for the future means increasing the range of our own reading. Thus, as we enter the sacred shelter ourselves, we can pull others into its safety as well.

Chapter 10

Like an Arrow in a Quiver

I heard Pat Boone tell of the time one of his daughters came home from school and announced, "My friends say I'm the only virgin in our class."

"How does that make you feel?" asked Pat.

She thought for a moment and said, "Kind of special."

Perhaps what she sensed was shelter at its best—the sense of being set apart, held in reserve for a special destiny, protected.

The opposite of this kind of shelter is found in the word *dissipated*. When you are dissipated your life and love are poured out in a dozen different directions prematurely and without focus, without intensity. You give yourself too early and too often without depth. Nothing is held in reserve and you lose the sense of feeling "kind of special." You lose that sense of being held in reserve for a special destiny.

"I once asked a class," says educator Allan Bloom, "how it could be that not too long ago parents would have said 'Never darken our door again' to wayward daughters, whereas now they rarely protest when boyfriends sleep over in their homes. A very nice, very normal young woman responded, 'Because it's no big deal.'" Bloom laments, "That says it all. This passionlessness is the most striking effect, or revelation, of the sexual revolution."[1]

Pastorally speaking, nothing agitates me more than seeing a gifted young woman throwing herself away on a man who is greatly inferior to her. In one case the lout was a long-haired, inarticulate drop-out and it was up to me to convey to the girl my grief at her choice. My task was a parental sort of thing. "You are special," I told her. "I believe God has a destiny for you that is great in every way. I just don't want you to do things now, to make decisions now, that will affect the rest of your life."

"You've been talking to my mother," she retorted. "You people just keep coming down on me all the time! I can't even think! I just want to scream!"

For a moment I thought she really would scream, right there in the Dairy Queen. I envisioned the scene that would cause—phone calls, police, reporters. "No!" I said. "I don't want to impose anything on you. I want you to be happy! Yes, I want you to be happy."

I thought she believed me when I reached out to her emotionally with a father's concern. I was, I suppose, acting in place of a father who was no longer there. All I *do* want is her happiness. And I know she isn't likely to be happy without shelter.

This is the sense that above all else we want to instill in all children: They are gifted. They are people of destiny. They must not cheapen their lives with decisions that are compromising, demeaning, dissipating. They must not abuse their bodies or their minds.

Teaching these precepts to our children is vital for their happiness. And it doesn't require us to at all times keep them on a short leash—under lock and key, so to speak. We must shelter them, but we must do it carefully. The term *sheltered upbringing* has stifled connotations. It suggests the denial of life that has pushed many a kid over the edge. But in its best sense, a sheltered upbringing saves a young life and strengthens it so that it can fly on its own. The great tragedy of today's society is that children lose innocence so young; they never experience the joy of preserving shelter.

Ruth and I try to govern the TV, give curfews, praise haircuts, and constantly inquire "Who were you with?" and "Where did you go?" We encourage reading; homework; regular meals; plenty of sleep; good hygiene; a clean room. You'd think a kid would get sick of it after awhile. And sometimes, to be truthful, our teenager sings the blues. He reminds us that all his friends' very godly parents are virtual libertarians compared to us ogres. But he has so many liberties within the boundaries of his rules that, in many ways, he leads the good life. He has access to a car that is practically his, fully furnished with a booming stereo. He has a keyboard . . . unlimited food, some money, friends. Thinking of his life brings to mind a hymn that seems to express what I think a preserving shelter should be: "There's a kindness in His justice which is more than liberty."[2]

Now that one of ours has left the nest, I find myself praying that this sense of being special will be reinforced. I pray for him along these lines: "Lord, bring people his way like Paul Little and Stanley Fish who have affected me so deeply. Bring him great people—professors, guest lecturers, authors, preachers—who will instill dreams of greatness in him. A real-life example speaks so much louder than simple words. Oh, bring him heroes, Lord, if you will!"

I visited his campus and found my prayer had been partially answered. A world-class expert on Bach had done a guest performance. "He kind of hummed while he played, Dad," Bob reported and began to imitate the bobbing motions of the longhaired guest. I suspected some musical eccentricity. Then Bob banged out the finest rendition of Bach I had heard in some time. "Pick me up in an hour," he said when I mentioned dinner. "I've got some practicing to do."

This idea of the arrow in the quiver, of being set apart for special things, relates to the Christian doctrine of sanctification. In fact, the word *sanctification* means "set apart." I have always liked the positive aspect of this, having endured more legalistic harangues along the way than most evangelicals. "Taste not," "touch not," "handle not"—we have our own versions of the Colossian heresy. But in its positive light, this business of being set apart is not so much a matter of being separated *from* as of being separated *unto*. Paul describes himself as "separated unto" the gospel of God, a positive movement *toward* God and his purposes.

A truly separated lifestyle is not a stilted deprived life that presumes to please God by its deprivations. On the contrary, it is a life devoted fully to God, the God of creation. This is a life in which God's life fills the inner reservoir and leaves little room for the fruitless, unhealthy vestiges of a life not worth living.

I have heard the life of a person set apart compared to the Pin Oak tree. It carries its leaves long after they have dried up, all through the winter and into the following spring, and it is a pathetic sight. It tenaciously holds to its precious old leaves. No amount of wintry blasts will drive them off. The Pin Oak only drops last year's growth as the new life of spring surges into its branches. So it is with our lives. No amount of negative injunction can remove the ugliness of the past. No amount of ecclesiastical hot air can sanctify us. But the fresh life of God, filling our inner lives to capacity, makes us truly separated unto him. We stretch out toward him and produce surprising, plentiful fresh growth. He makes us holy in the most marvelous way.

The idea that we are like arrows in a quiver intended for a special destiny comes from Isaiah:

> *The Lord called Me from the womb,*
> *From the body of my mother He named Me.*
> *And He has made My mouth like a sharp sword;*
> *In the shadow of His hand He has concealed Me,*
> *And He has also made Me a select arrow;*
> *He has hidden Me in His quiver* (Isa. 49:1–2 NASV).

The master archer prepares his select arrows with great care. First he chooses them and then polishes and hones them. Finally, he places them in his quiver where they'll be protected until he needs to use them. That is how a man should see his life. All of his training and the years of schooling contribute to his polishing and honing. That is the way Isaiah saw his life. He knew there is no substitute for good training. Isaiah's influence was due largely to his erudite upbringing. His training made it possible for him to walk into the courts of kings and be comfortable. It made him a select arrow.

These days education has fallen on hard times. We aggrandize school drop-outs who made it big as though leaving school was part of the reason for their success. "Our speaker today has . . . (built America's fastest-growing church, as it turned out) without finishing seminary!" That was the introduction. Bill Hybels rose to speak and said, "Well, it's not as though I *couldn't* have finished." I thought it was exactly right. We may opt to postpone training, defer it indefinitely under the constraints of a higher calling, but don't make that choice sound like a strategic one.

Education and training are part of our honing and polishing. They help make us ready for our special destinies. But it seems we are fascinated with God's desire to bless rustics. He pulled Amos from sheepherding and made him a powerful prophet to Samaria. He pulled Simon Peter from his fishing boat and made him a mighty apostle. These examples of God's unlimited greatness fascinate us. We have a tendency, some of us, to think we don't need to do much ourselves. God will make everything happen right—give us uncommon insight and wisdom—when his time is right.

But God also uses well-trained people. For every Amos, there is an Isaiah. For every rustic, there is a Moses. For every Peter, a Paul. Thank God. If all the world were ill-trained prophet types, where would the sanity be? I love to see a polished arrow now and then, committed scholars who train young people to grasp both the Scriptures and their times with integrity. These are some of the select arrows in God's quiver. They take dead aim and hit with great force.

One of the great things about training is the sense of comfort it provides. It gives a sheltered feeling that I esteem very highly. You develop an ease in sharing concepts and are comfortable with the interchange of ideas between disciplines. "Thoroughly prepared for the Master's use"—this is the great ideal.

The greatest preparation we can make is to *live* like people of destiny, offering our best selves to our times. We must carefully preserve our bodies and minds through discipline and study, and we must instill this sense in the generation that follows. We must cherish our hiddenness. God conceals in his hand those he desires to use. There would have been no triumphal ministry in Galilee, where the people in darkness saw a great light, without the hidden years in Nazareth. Paul could not have stood before kings without the hidden years in the Arabian deserts. Our strength stems from our hiddenness, our effectiveness from our disciplined training. Preserved within the quiver of God's destiny, we give the Holy Spirit lives that he can use.

Chapter 11

With the Illusion of Privacy

The human desire for secret hiding places can produce lifestyles that are ungodly. Money is often a factor. It can provide a secret place, an escape that insulates you from the racket of everyday life. But such shelter is not all it seems. It is not necessarily good. If it is an escape without an enfolding, merely an insulation from life's hard knocks and there is no inner warmth, it isn't true shelter. Unless the inner life is rich, this hiding place is merely lonely isolation.

We think of "exclusive living" as ideal and make it synonymous with "the good life," and all over the world people who can afford it indulge in this kind of shelter. Detached people in their private enclaves, hidden away, ignorant of the plight of the world's poor—this produces an isolation from the mass of mankind that is almost dehumanizing. Exclusive lifestyles can be excuses, and poor ones, for self-indulgence.

It seems strange and paradoxical, but a true shelter is only given those who are committed to others. Isaiah said it is those who remove the yoke and give themselves to the hungry who are "like a watered garden" and will "raise up the age old foundations." They are the "repairers of the breach" (see Isa. 58:9–12). It is the one who "walks righteously, speaks with sincerity," and "rejects unjust gain" who will "dwell on high" and have as his refuge "the impregnable rock" (Isa. 33:16).

But those who "deprive the needy of justice" and "rob the poor . . . of their rights, in order that widows may be their spoil, and that they may plunder the orphans" will "crouch among the victims" and "fall among the slain" (see Isa. 10:1–4). Even God's sanctuary does not welcome the "trampling of courts" with "worthless offerings" by those who do not "seek justice, reprove the ruthless, defend the orphan and plead for the widow" (see Isa. 1:12–17).

Such people live in an illusion of shelter. They may be hidden from men, but God ferrets them out. One should never say, "My way is hidden from the Lord," for there *is* no secret place to hide from him. He is "the Creator of the ends of the earth . . . his understanding is inscrutable" (Isa. 40:28). Those who have "made falsehood their refuge" and "concealed themselves with deception" will find that their lives are measured with a measuring line of justice and a level of righteousness. "The hail will sweep away the refuge of lies, and the waters shall overflow the hiding place" (Isa. 28:17).

Secluded havens are not new. Isaiah warned against them long ago. "Woe to those who join house to house . . . until there is no more room . . . to live alone in the midst of the land." He warned, "In my hearing the Lord of hosts said, 'Truly many houses shall be desolate, great and beautiful ones without inhabitants'" (5:8–9).

Ancient Judah was like its prime minister, Shebna, who planned his comfortable future right through to a nestled resting place on a hillside. God spoke to him through his prophet and said, "What have you here and whom have you here, that you have hewn a sepulcher here, as he who hews himself a sepulcher on high, who carves a tomb for himself in a rock?" What awaits this self-indulgent public official is something quite different from the secluded resting place he has designed for, "The Lord will throw you away violently, O mighty man . . . and toss you like a ball into a large country; there you shall die. . . . I will drive you out of your office, and from your position he will pull you down" (Isa. 22:15–19).

Like the nation as a whole, this official had turned inward on himself. Rather than serving the needy, he served his own interests in the most thorough way. He hewed and cut a prominent memorial for himself. The passage repeats the word *here* as though to say *here* of all places, perhaps on the prominent hillside east of David's city where many fine rock-cut tombs have been found, *here* you do not belong.

The worst time to meet a prophet is when you are building a memorial for yourself, especially if the nation is in such bad shape it is about to be scattered to the four winds. This prominent official was in for a surprise. Rather than in his sheltered resting place on the hillside, he would be flung out like an unclean thing and die in ignominy in a foreign land, a "wide land" like Assyria with its broad plains. The man who planned a sheltered end would die of the harshest exposure.

Shebna's story concludes a chapter that describes the exposure of Judah. It was a nation that had flocked to the rooftops either to party or to share fragments of what good news there was. And this nation was more exposed than she knew. While she was full of loud "rejoicing and gladness" over some favorable break in the Assyrian pressure against her, the celebratory feasts and wine were hardly justified. Isaiah saw beyond temporary respite to imminent catastrophe: "All your rulers have fled together; they are captured by the archers. All who are found in you are bound together, who have fled from afar" (Isa. 22:3). It is as though the people were in a "valley of vision," seeing only their immediate circumstances (see Isa. 22:1). *Que sera, sera,* they said, eat and drink for tomorrow we die. The fatalism of their attitude was unforgivable as far as Isaiah was concerned. There was no covering for their sin: "It was revealed in my hearing . . . that this iniquity will be no atonement for you even to your death" (Isa. 22:14).

These ancient figures have a modern look. Our world is full of Shebnas, from New York City to Guatemala City, who focus on their own seclusion and comfort quite apart from the needs of their people. When powerful people live in private isolation from the hurts of their world, the desperate urgency of the times does not reach them. Opulent private villas that can only be entered by permission, secluded country estates surrounded by fences and alarm systems, huge mansions behind walls on closed-off streets—this is where the rich and powerful are usually tucked away.

A good part of the church has followed suit. Many congregations have found a niche in the suburbs quite removed from the plight of most cities. No fear of vagrants, muggers, unsightly visitors, they are the suburban churches. But, as Gibson Winter reminds us, we are made ineffective by our suburban captivity. Not only that, but the membership hides in their own enclaves, if they can afford it. Very private streets are preferred for housing: a "close," a "crescent," or a "way"—any place that is *away* from the rowdy populace and its needs.

Yet we are called to identify with the plight of the ravaged and broken, not to hide from it. What kind of people do we become when we hide ourselves from the victims of our society? *Secluded, exclusive, reclusive*—we can become unbalanced, unproductive monuments before our time. On the other hand, the people who risk the most exposure provide some of our best examples of truly sheltered lives. When Albert Schweitzer visited America, for example, he was asked why he would travel on the train third class. He answered, "Because there is no fourth class!" Perhaps Richard Foster has best expressed the way to find true shelter.

> We have failed to see . . . this amazing paradox: true self-fulfillment comes only through self-denial. There is no other way. The most certain way to miss self-fulfillment is to pursue it. . . . A blazing God-consciousness frees us from self-consciousness. It is freedom. It is joy. It is life.[1]

We experience shelter most intensely as we give ourselves for others. Shelter, like joy and love, slips away when we become too compulsive about it. It comes to us as a gift when our commitment is to endure some hardships on behalf of others. Shelter at its best comes in the midst of life, not apart from life. It is a pocket of peace in the midst of the storm.

Part 4

Shelter and Ceremony

Ceremonies lend solemnity to life. What comfort we find in them. They have the majestic concept of covenant that brings us into contact with a power greater than ourselves in building relationships. Covenant relationships stabilize and protect our lives. Being true to a covenant keeps things solid when emotions are giving way. On the other hand, we experience painful exposure from the tearing down of the ceremonial and a loss of the sense of shelter it brings. That is why the ceremonies of everyday life as well as those that occur only on special occasions are important. In a way they replace the snow forts of my youth. They are consoling shelters.

Some of my forts are grand dining rooms with tinkling silverware, lovely aromas, and white linen. Waiters in tuxedos move softly among dark paneled walls, hot biscuits and rolls are served before you see the menu, little delicacies for dessert are included with the meal, and all the while a pianist plays. The imposing elegance of the place creates a kind of hush, almost a reverential feel. Grand dining rooms are expensive, but we need to visit one now and then. We need to nourish that part of us that needs ceremony. No matter how tawdry and banal the stuff of daily life, one can still preserve the ideal of elegance.

This is perhaps the spirit of a Thoreau, who refused to live "meanly." Critic Robert Bly observes:

> Living meanly, to Thoreau, is the opposite of "living sincerely." To live sincerely is to live your own life, not your father's life or your mother's life or your neighbor's life; to spend soul on large concerns, not to waste your life as a kind of human ant carrying around small burdens. . . . To live sincerely is to "live deep and suck out all the marrow of life." . . . That may require unsociability.[1]

Some of my forts remind me that there is this higher life.

In an essay on equality, C. S. Lewis argues that we must retain an inner sense of hierarchy:

> There is no spiritual sustenance in flat equality. . . . We begin to breed that stunted and envious sort of mind which hates all superiority. The man who cannot conceive a joyful and loyal obedience on the one hand, nor an unembarrassed and noble acceptance of that obedience on the other . . . is a prosaic barbarian. . . . Under the necessary coverings of legal equality, the whole hierarchial dance and harmony of our deep and joyously accepted spiritual inequalities should be alive. . . . Hierachy within can alone preserve egalitarianism without.[2]

I have known a little elegance to work miracles for the people I live with; so much so, that I like to insist on it when I detect mean-spiritedness in someone close to me. I prescribe a touch of elegance and savor the results. My staff, my colleagues and friends, my wife—I have seen their spirits expand after such a time.

Clothing is also part of this kind of shelter. Obviously clothes do more than cover our bodies, although the pathetic plight of refugees reminds us of the basic role of clothes. Without them, obviously, people are cold. But our clothes also make statements about us. They provide a vehicle through which we can, if we choose, express something of our spirit. And they can facilitate a certain acceptance and respect; in short, a kind of shelter for the spirit that is very accessible if not inexpensive. Sometimes all it takes is a fresh approach to clothing to make you feel downright invincible.

You are warm, unthreatened, engaging, gregarious, and kind. What has come over you? You feel strong because you look good. Your body tells you that.

Ceremonial dining, expressive clothing—these are ceremonies for the body as well as the spirit, but there are other ceremonies that mostly shelter the spirit. I walked into our softly lit church one bitter night during winter. What a sanctuary it was to me. My body soaked up its warm fragrance and I found myself singing the familiar hymn: "How lovely is your dwelling place, Almighty God; there's a hunger deep inside my soul; only in your presence are my heart and flesh restored; how lovely is your dwelling place."[3] And then to be part of a larger whole, a corporate vigil of prayer that led some 200 people through twenty-four hours of intercession—how consoling it was to be thus sheltered by the body of Christ, the Church.

We all have shelter readily available in the ceremonies of life. There is no need to be completely bereft of ceremony, even in the most primitive or informal setting. We can build on our preferences and we can create our own ceremonies. We can infuse life with dignity and due process. As we do, we can stare down the unruly tumult of our time.

Chapter 12

Sanctuaries

Our church is divided, in a friendly sort of way, over the hymn-book. We have not taken to hurling them yet, but the lines are clearly drawn. The problem might well be described as a conflict between the "baby-boomers" and their elders. One group favors contemporary choruses shown on an overhead screen; the other prefers traditional hymns in four-part congregational harmony. Our congregation is composed of both groups and fairly evenly divided between them. Our board members have equal preferences, too. So if we took to hurling hymnals it would be a fairly even contest.

This issue is a symptom of a larger one that has to do with worship style and, indeed, the whole concept of the worship service. Is it to be primarily reverential with a certain stately decorum, or should worship services be primarily celebratory with God's people exulting freely in their Lord?

I believe there is room for both. There is room for the overhead projector beaming worship choruses and a congregation on its feet, lifting praise with joy and enthusiasm. And there is room for "Speak, Lord, in the stillness while I wait for Thee" sung to the stately tones of the organ.

I hear from both camps, of course. "You keep singing those old hymns, Pastor; that's what we need," or "Pastor, let's scrap that hymnbook and allow more freedom for the Spirit to move; we are heading the way of the other denominations . . . mere ritual." I try to be responsive to both sides. For example, I will launch a typical worship service with a hymn and move swiftly into a succession of related Scripture choruses. I try to provide a musical setting for both celebration and reverential awe. I want the people to both look up and bow down.

Yet, I too have drawn a line. I will not tolerate racket. I will not cross the parameters of reasonable time. I will not make people physically uncomfortable by having them on their feet forever. I *like* a bit of ritual. Also, I have aged just a little bit, and I like a little quiet more than I used to.

I like what a young mother said recently. We were taking a moment for shared life in a worship service. "I've just come from a very stressful situation," she said, and then her voice gave out. Her expression of helplessness told me she could not describe the experience. Eventually she was able to whisper, "This place really is a refuge."

It is a refuge for Doris too, who just lost her husband. She sits with me in a quiet room off the sanctuary and weeps her way through her shocking loss. All of the regret, the loneliness, the pain—she needs a sheltered place just to begin to express some of that.

For others, our church is not refuge enough. One man wants primarily the stillness of sanctuary. He is a soft-spoken artist who is also musical. Though he retains his membership with us, he passes some Sunday mornings down at an old, crumbling church in the center of town. He loves the ancient dark sanctuary with its refracted light and squeaky floors; he likes the simplicity of the mostly senior congregants who follow a carefully arranged order of service. He loves the pipe organ. Secretly, I wish I could go with him now and then. It sounds like a choice old fort to me.

But I am committed to my suburban church with its modern lines, vast expanse of white across ceiling and walls, carpet and padding to the right of us, to the left of us, and beneath us like shaggy brown everlasting arms. And its livelier sounds. We can create a fortress feeling with some small changes here and there:

more of a pipe sound on the organ, better use of lighting and decor. My pet project is to remove all fluorescents and replace them with indirect lighting that can be either bright or dim at the turn of a knob. I'd like a messenger phone by my right hand: "Dim the lights, boys, if you will." In either an ancient dark sanctuary or a modern bright one we can have a profound silent moment that gives the Spirit an opportunity to search our hearts.

Recently, I visited an older, traditional church, which imparted an awesome sense of refuge. It was in a small town in Ontario. The building looked historic; it probably went up before the town hall. There was such a strong sense of God there. Afterward I asked our friends about the service. One found it "just plain dull."

"I found it," I said, "meaningfully dull: the long readings of scripture, the interlacing of prayer that covered national and global issues in some detail, the simplicity of ancient hymns sung to the pipe organ—all of it touched an important chord with me."

"But you leave unchanged," our friend said.

"Not necessarily," I contended. "And even so, all kinds of people leave all kinds of churches unchanged."

I had to think about what I would add to such a service. I loved the reverential tone and the structure of the worship. But I sensed my friend was on to something. It had to do with congregational response, I think. The readings and prayers seemed to lack the personal, heart-and-soul commitment that true worship requires: response to receive Christ, response to offer ourselves to the Lord again, a demonstration of commitment.

"The people have to meet God," my father used to say. This was in the context of an up-tempo Pentecostal church he pastored, a church with country and western leanings. It was a mismatch, to be sure—my stately, tasteful father and that down-home church. But he focused on the encounter moment and enjoyed his ministry there. In fact, there was a touch of renewal in that congregation that my parents still love to talk about years later.

We should emphasize a time of response. It is after proclamation that congregational praise is best. In the moments anticipating dismissal, I like time for extended praise, celebration, and whole-hearted commitment.

"Praise and worship" seminars have become somewhat vogue in our town. Across town recently there was a seminar that generated great corporate praise, a sweep of exuberant charismatic expression that brought most of the house into united worship. As the evening went along, impromptu songs of worship inspired considerable clapping and dancing and all the physical expressions of praise that people find in scripture. Guitars and a drum backed up electronic keyboards to provide sustained rhythm. It was "a praise happening" and a truly exhilarating experience.

We usually think of *worship* as a quiet inward experience and *praise* as an exuberant outward experience. But I had a quiet worship experience during the seminar that was filled also with praise. A cluster of people had gathered in a small Sunday school classroom for a worship on publishing songs. We opened with a quiet worship moment. Then the leader, who had set up his keyboard, led us in the chorus "Let There Be Glory." Some people consider this chorus a bit of an anthem and leap to their feet at the first note, but we sang it in a very mellow way while seated.

> Let there be glory and honor and praise,
> Glory and honor to Jesus,
> Glory, honor,
> Glory and honor to Him.[1]

While we sang, the room was flooded with the strongest sense of God's presence. It was a choice moment of encounter. It reminded me of Elijah's "still small voice" (see 1 Kings 19:12). God was not in the wind, the earthquake, or the fire, and he certainly was not in the bass guitar. He was in a gentle whisper. And that is where I find him most.

For Isaiah, the sanctuary was a blessed refuge. He described how a threatened king, Hezekiah, tore his clothes in desperation over the impending Assyrian assault, "and went into the house of the Lord" (Isa. 37:1). It was there that he had the space he needed: he spread the letter of ultimatum before God and offered his classic prayer.

O Lord of hosts, God of Israel, the One who dwells between the cherubim, You are God You alone of all the kingdoms of the

*earth. You have made heaven and earth. Incline Your ear, O
Lord, and hear; open Your eyes, O Lord, and see; and hear all
the words of Sennacherib, who has sent to reproach the living
God. . . . Now therefore, O Lord our God, save us from his
hand, that all the kingdoms of the earth may know that You are
the Lord, You alone.* (Isa. 37:16–20)

In a later passage, Isaiah described the temple specifically in
those terms: "My house shall be called a house of prayer for all
nations" (Isa. 56:7). It was a definition that our Lord himself used
against the debased and bawdy temple of his day. "You have made
it a den of thieves," he protested, and he drove out the offending
merchants.

Isaiah did not address transgressions of the sanctity of the temple; he spoke to those who felt unworthy of it, those who felt disin-
herited. Foreigners and eunuchs without families were encouraged
to find a supportive community in the sanctuary:

> *Do not let the son of the foreigner*
> *Who has joined himself to the Lord*
> *Speak, saying,*
> *"The Lord has utterly separated me from His people";*
> *Nor let the eunuch say,*
> *"Here I am, a dry tree."*
> *For . . . to them I will give in My house*
> *And within My walls a place and a name*
> *Better than that of sons and daughters;*
> *I will . . . make them joyful in My house of prayer.*
>   (Isa. 56:3–7)

People still need the shelter of the church more than any other
kind. The refugee who has fled the turmoil of a Latin American
homeland; the courageous immigrant who has left a well-paid career in Singapore to secure new educational opportunities for his
children; the person without family—these seem to prize the
church with special affection. And they contribute the most ardor
to its life.

There is nothing half-hearted about the Vena family. They came to us from Chile. As a government worker, Luis had seen the country through the turmoil of both the Allende and Pinochet regimes. Then it was time to leave. He ended up in our town, thousands of miles from his homeland, missing Santiago, family and friends.

"I suffered so much for two years," he says of the culture shock he and his young family went through. "It was a very bad time. . . . But it was also very good." Luis touches his heart and confesses that God used his grief times to draw him closer. The church was accepting and helpful during the time of adjustment. And now, everything about the church, which in a sense is his country, is sacred. Prayer time is vocal and intense; worship is wholehearted. He draws full value from his sanctuary.

Vena reminds me of some lonely, lost times of my own and how the church provided refuge. I had no need for hype. I just wanted to be among God's people and hear the strong word of scripture to feel the comfort of God's touch. Like Luis, I have grown spiritually during some times that were painfully lonely. God graciously met me when, as a teen-ager on my own for a time, I reached out to him in the prayer room of the London Gospel Temple. I remember clearly the strong consolation of the Lutheran Seminary chapel when my plans were frustrated. Feeling victimized, very tired, distended, I was strengthened as the all male gathering lifted up a great hymn, to a poorly-played pipe organ:

> "Every joy or trial falleth from above,
> Traced upon our dial, by the Son of love;
> We may trust him fully all for us to do;
> They who trust him wholly, find him wholly true."[2]

My thesis, in Seminary, was on "The Servanthood of the Church." Like any self-respecting seminarian in the seventies, I inveighed against the church's walls. "The church is the extension of the incarnation," I argued. "As such it must extend the servanthood of Jesus." I built around a great quote of Jamaican William Watty's: "Until North American Christians are willing to forsake their luxuries and follow their Lord among the poor and oppressed, they will neither deserve nor receive a hearing for the gospel." We were all calling on the church to tear down its walls and become more of a servant to humanity. And that great note still needs to be sounded. The church must be scattered like salt and light in the world. But the church must also be gathered. And that gathering, in reverence, is as fine a shelter as you can find.

On a trip to Romania I observed two young women whose differences point up the gathering the church needs to be doing. The young prostitute was usually there strolling in front of Timisoira's Central Hotel, a bouquet of red roses in hand, her pimp alongside. Something in the sidelong look of her eyes conveyed a sadness beyond comprehension, a depth of despair. Romania gets a lot of male visitors in the summer from neighboring countries, because girls are "cheap" in Romania, like most things. This girl certainly looks cheap. She walks the cobblestone street, outrageously made up in a leopard-skin outfit that is far beyond erotic. It is garish, the stuff of burlesque. But this is tragic reality in Romania.

Later that day, another young woman walked across the front of a church sanctuary, violin in hand. She had been asked to do a recital in front of her orchestra while we, the unexpected audience of visitors, reclined in the comfortable pews while we waited for dinner. It was a beautiful moment after a long day on the streets: the cool, dimly lit sanctuary, the young artist surrounded by her approving colleagues, the plaintive Russian melody, the prospects of dinner in a friendly church that had kindly agreed to feed our ministry team during our few days in town.

Perhaps they were the same age, the prostitute and the violinist. They were in the same town and the same troubled nation—how could the course of their lives be so different? One was headed toward an early grave, it seemed, on a street that would end abruptly in violence or terminal illness. The other, in Christ, was on what the song calls "a street that never ends."

How different their surroundings. One was surrounded by the filth of that street with its iron grates over the windows, broken-down curbs, a sidewalk with cracks so deep you wondered how spiked heels could make progress on them, the old museum on the other side that looked more like a rat-infested warehouse. The other woman was surrounded by the sanctity of the church. The wholesomeness of this environment was almost tangible after a day on those streets.

One had hands that clutched roses; the other, hands that held a violin. In the one case, the hands probably had never learned a skill, had never been held in love, had never been led. In the other case, a young violinist had the well-trained hands of a musician. Perhaps she had learned the prayer we put to music, "make my hands like those of skilled musicians." Those fingers worked their way up and down the neck of the instrument with a competence produced by years of practice.

The streetwalker had no home, it seemed. She was out on the cobblestone late into the night and, sure enough, she was there first thing in the morning. Can she live on those streets? On the other hand, the violinist went "home" after the rehearsal. We went to dinner and on to our "homes." The orchestra went "home." Everyone went home, except the one who needed "home" the most. I thought of Jesus' invitation, "Come unto me, all who are weary and heavy-laden, and I will give you rest" (Matt. 11:28, NASV). The weariness of living on those streets was beyond my comprehension.

One young woman has no song. If she ever had a song, it is now crushed and stamped out by life, long buried in ashes. The other, contributes a melody to the world. It is a beautiful indigenous melody that rises out of her eastern culture in praise to the Lord of all creation. We often prayed that the "new song" of salvation, carried in joyful street evangelism to the cities of Romania, might penetrate even the most darkened and silent heart.

The one girl had no helper, no instructor, no examiner. Pimps and beggars, the coarsest and basest of men, surrounded her all the time. Her world was nightmarish. But the violinist was surrounded by the Christian community: a conductor who evaluated her progress, a team of colleagues who tapped their bows approvingly after the recital, encouragers, enablers, all of them. This is the church. It lifts a life. It enables people to be what they can be. It places a divine seal on a life.

To me it seemed a matter of life and death. One poor young

woman walks the streets in spiritual death. "She that lives in plea-sure is dead while she lives," writes Paul (1 Tim. 5:6). Physical death seems imminent. Eternal death awaits. What a specter she is of the great issues involved in the paths we choose. The other young woman has life—a life of commitment, of service, of fulfil-ment, abundant life. She seemed to show what it is to pass from death unto life.

The two scenes spoke of the elevating power of the gospel. It is "the power of God unto salvation," Paul writes (Rom. 1:16). It turns a life that is cheap and worthless and bent on survival into a contributor, one who pours harmony and beauty into the world. It transforms a life from being an object to being a person with some-thing to give. It lifts life from the gutter. It surrounds a life with a caring community. It frees one from the sin and passions that cheapen life and deem it worthless. The gospel puts supreme value on life. It gives life worth. We see our worth in Christ, in the great love of the Father in sending his Son into the world. The gospel does not allow us to question our value. We can say, "For God so loved *me* that he gave his only begotten Son . . ." How urgently does our broken world need this gospel!

The two scenes also reminded me of the sanctifying influence of the church as sanctuary. The church provides a wholesome envi-ronment where a life can rise above the level of base physicality. The church is a place that appreciates spiritual qualities above all else. It is a place where our bodies are offered as "instruments of righteousness."

Throughout Romania, we had seen the church doing just that. *Pace Domnule,* "Peace of the Lord," the brethren said as we en-tered their sanctuaries. And we sensed the peace in their lives. This church is strong on decorum and decency: women and men on opposite sides, for the most part, married women modestly entering with a head covering. Sometimes a service seemed regi-mented. But then there was the bursting into fervent corporate prayer where one felt the pulsebeat of this church's life. Large or small, urban or rural—the churches of Romania provide a new kind of life to people, an atmosphere of worship and growth. They give a chance to lives that badly need one.

I walk softly within the walls of my sanctuary. I dim the lights and savor the refuge that is the church:

He who dwells in the secret place of the Most High
Shall abide under the shadow of the Almighty.
I will say of the Lord, "He is my refuge and my fortress;
My God, in Him I will trust." (Ps. 91:1-2)

I feel the beauty of its strong walls.

The church was such a warm retreat on a recent frosty night, providing the setting for a small group of us to lift up the psalm in a lovely modern melody:

How lovely is your dwelling place
O Lord Almighty!
My soul yearns, even faints,
for the courts of the Lord;
my heart and my flesh cry out
for the living God.
Even the sparrow has found a home, and the
swallow a nest for herself,
where she may have her young—
A place near your altar. . . .
Better is one day in your courts
than a thousand elsewhere.
(Ps. 84:1-10 NIV)

The nesting theme, drawn from birds which the psalmist saw around the temple precincts, reminds us of home, of nourishment, of a sheltered environment for growth. This too is the church: a place to feel, a place to be, at home.

Chapter 13

Clothed

"**W**herewithal shall ye be clothed?" as Jesus said, has become one of life's great preoccupations. But who would have thought that clothes would become such an obsession? It is not the basic shelter of clothing that preoccupies us, of course. That we take for granted. We worry about the kind of statement our clothes make about us. Do they convey us as *progressive,* for example? The advertisers assure us that to be out of step with fashion is to be *out of step,* period. Your label is either theirs or "old-fashioned." You are sure to be seen as regressive and unwilling to change.

Clothing can also make a statement about status. People who are willing to pay any price to wear "the best" must have, we are assured, some money to throw around. Expensive designer clothing helps make that kind of statement.

And clothing also has enormous potential for sex appeal. The designers assure us that a transformation takes place the minute you slip into their latest garb: A flabby body becomes something like the lean, well-proportioned mannequin that models clothing in the stores. If only it were so! Think of the hours of sweaty fitness pursuits we would be spared.

All of this is a multi-million dollar industry, of course. People are almost as concerned about what they wear as with how they get around. Dress is one of our great passions.

Apparently clothing was an obsession in Isaiah's time too. The prevailing concern with fashion and finery sounds remarkably like what we find in a modern newspaper:

> *The daughters of Zion are haughty,*
> *And walk with outstretched necks*
> *And wanton eyes,*
> *Walking and mincing as they go,*
> *Making a jingling with their feet.*
> (Isa. 3:16)

In that culture as in ours, clothing made a statement about status. It distinguished these women from the lower classes. Unfortunately, the finery of Zion's women was at the expense of the poor. It is one thing for clothes to make a statement about you, but that statement should not be that you are indifferent to the poor. Isaiah warned the women that God was not pleased with them: "The plunder from the poor is in your houses. What do you mean by crushing My people and grinding the face of the poor?" (Isa. 3:14–15).

The prophet Isaiah is so outraged by the statement these women were making that he pronounced a fiery judgment:

> *In that day the Lord will take away the finery;*
> *The jingling anklets, the scarves, and the crescents;*
> *The pendants, the bracelets, and the veils;*
> *The headdresses, the leg ornaments, and the headbands;*
> *The perfume boxes, the charms, and the rings;*
> *The nose jewels, the festive apparel, and the mantles;*
> *The outer garments, the purses, and the mirrors;*
> *The fine linen, the turbans, and the robes.*
>
> *And so it shall be:*
> *Instead of a sweet smell there will be a stench;*
> *Instead of a sash, a rope;*
> *Instead of well-set hair, baldness;*
> *Instead of a rich robe, a girding of sackcloth;*
> *And branding instead of beauty.* (Isa. 3:18–24)

Not only do clothes make a statement, they should make the *right* statement.

Probably our fashion pages make a similar statement about this society. The newspaper that devotes some ten pages to fashion news gives only a half page to the plight of the naked: close to one million Kurdish refugees on the Turkish/Iraqi border. While we look to clothing to enhance our self-images and enjoy what it can do for us psychologically, the poor of the earth reach out to it just for warmth.

Global disparity of these proportions gives added weight to the words of Peter: "And let not your adornment be merely external— braiding the hair and wearing gold jewelry, or putting on dresses; but let it be the hidden person of the heart, with the imperishable quality of a gentle and quiet spirit, which is precious in the sight of God" (1 Pet. 3:3–4 NASV). The apostle says to focus on inner beauty. We may dress to knock them dead in the streets. But is it possible that inner nakedness, inner rags, may underlie our natty exteriors?

Isaiah points us to the most important fashion of all—call it inner fashion, when he speaks of receiving a crown of beauty instead of ashes, the oil of gladness instead of mourning, and a garment of praise instead of a spirit of despair (see Isa. 61:3). This is the inner clothing that God alone gives. And he bestows it freely on the brokenhearted, the poor, the captive. This inner clothing is the result of the Messiah's work:

> *The Spirit of the Lord GOD is upon me,*
> *Because the LORD has anointed to me*
> *To preach good tidings to the poor.* (Isa. 61:1)

That Jesus should assign such a passage to himself lends it particular weight. His gracious work is to clothe us inwardly when we are destitute.

This great shelter of inner clothing is eloquently expressed in verse 10 of chapter 61:

> *I will greatly rejoice in the LORD,*
> *My soul shall be joyful in my God;*
> *For he has clothed me with the garments of salvation,*
> *He has covered me with the robe of righteousness,*

As a bridegroom decks himself with ornaments,
And as a bride adorns herself with her jewels.

There is a marvelous sense of worth conveyed in this clothing. It makes one feel like a bridegroom, a priest, or like the bride herself. This is the distinction of clothing at its best. It sets the wearer apart. It has a "distinctive look." It is absolutely free, yet it is the costliest garb of all. It is the very robe of righteousness that covers all our sin.

Clothes have power. A culture like ours is swayed by the very powerful fashion industry. And when you and I slip into something well-fitting, beautifully designed and new, we have a fresh sense of power. Not only do we cover our bodies, we shelter our spirits from the contempt we sense for the ill-clad. A meticulously-dressed person feels somehow impervious. It is no wonder we are fascinated with fashion.

Maybe all we can ask is that we moderate our fascination with clothes by asking ourselves some questions: What kind of statement do my clothes make about me? I enjoy the psychological lift they can give me. Can I do so without forgetting that the world is full of people who need clothes for basic warmth? Is my enjoyment of the latest fashion at the expense of those who need clothing, the most basic of all shelters? Can I match what I spend on clothes for myself with what I give to the unclothed? How is my inner wardrobe? Is it possible that I try to conceal inner rags with outer fashion? Can I perhaps match the time I spend shopping in the malls and catalogues with time spent working on my inner wardrobe of righteousness, praise, and a gentle spirit?

Chapter 14

Bound by a Covenant

Carmen was married at age thirty-eight to twenty-one-year-old Rose Marie and what a wedding it was. He wanted the ceremony to be perfect and planned everything well in advance. He submitted a full wedding ceremony for my approval, complete with communion, candlelighting, and the kind of theological overtones he wanted. He took charge of the rehearsal in a way I have not seen in more than fifty marriages—hushing the bridesmaids, threatening the ushers, coaxing Andrew the ring-bearer, and Christine the flower-girl, calling for another rehearsal "once more for good measure." Through it all, Carmen—a true professional—maintained an affable smile, allowing himself a laugh here and a kiss there.

At the reception, where most grooms would find themselves awkward, pallid, and nervous, Carmen was perfectly at ease. He kissed the bride with aplomb when called upon, delivered a witty, sincere speech to his new family's young sisters and brother-in-law, who he "honestly cared about as good friends," and his own parents, who should regret "not one thing." He moved about with the glowing bride to distribute cake and led the ceremonial first dance. What a performance! I found myself wishing that all grooms would wait until they were old enough to know what they were doing. Throughout the planning and counseling sessions, it was clear that nothing had escaped him. This bride could relax. All would be well and it was.

Carmen had followed me to the altar in his gray tuxedo, a groomed and polished man, complete with puffy shirt cuffs and a pink carnation, glancing approvingly at his groomsmen as they filed in to join him. He offered his arm to his bride in a strong yet gentle way as her nervous father groped for a seat. He knelt for the emblems reverently and responded clearly to the "wilt thous."

But when we were just nicely into the vows I saw his composure fail, and heard his voice catch. He had to turn his eyes away from the lovely bride's and look sideways at me while he repeated his vows, his voice suddenly very hushed on the words he had personally composed: "To help you develop your personal potential . . . all my love as long as we both . . ." To see Carmen hushed with deep emotion was quite moving. My own eyes got a bit misty, I believe. Then Carmen prayed and all the authority fled from his voice. He whispered a broken prayer like Luke's publican, humbly asking God for wisdom and strength and steadfast love. It was a tender, quiet moment, the stuff of great weddings. It was enough to cause the most jaded cynic to break down. It was a covenant for a lifetime.

No matter how often you hear them, wedding ceremonies convey something about covenant agreements. And what a great, solidifying influence they are, these agreements, in an age which cares more about keeping your plants than about keeping your word. We have contracts, of course, with limited liability and some built-in loopholes to provide escape from the terms as needed. But the marriage covenant, with its implications of unlimited liability, unflinching commitment and loyalty, even unto death—this is language that is largely foreign to us.

No matter how weak it seems the marriage covenant has become, these covenant agreements can provide us with our greatest shelters. It is not that we are so idealistic about the marriage covenant that we deny the harsh realities of our time concerning the escalating divorce rate, violence in the home, and the breakdown of family life. But entering a lifelong covenant relationship with a person brings with it enormous strength.

"How do you like being a married student this year?" I asked Bev, a newlywed nursing student.

"Oh, I'm so relaxed," she said. "I don't know how I ever made it on my own."

I watch her and Gary, both full-time students, discovering that two can live *better* than one when the ingredients are right. Their commitment to each other is nurtured by a shared faith and a shared vision of life in service. They appear to me to be much more confident and self-assured than they were before their vows. They seem to provide live evidence of the words of Ecclesiastes: "Two are better than one because they have a good reward for their labor. For if they fall, one will lift up his companion" (Eccl. 4:9–10).

How is it that marriage at its best carries such strength? Perhaps it lies in the fact that God is a covenant-maker throughout scripture and he honors our covenants with his presence and strength. His faithfulness and undying love are demonstrated as he enters these solemn agreements: "Now behold, I Myself do establish My covenant with you, and with your descendants after you; and with every living creature that is with you . . . and all flesh shall never again be cut off by the water of the flood, neither shall there again be a flood to destroy the earth" (Gen. 9:9–11).

Abraham also witnessed God's desire to enter covenant relations: "I will establish my covenant between Me and you and your descendants after you throughout their generations for an everlasting covenant, to be God to you and to your descendants. . . . And I will give to you . . . all the land of Canaan, for an everlasting possession" (Gen. 17:7–8). Adam, Noah, Abraham, Moses, David, all heard God express his covenant commitment to man.

In Isaiah God is the covenant-maker whose commitment to his people endures long after political upheaval and moral failure have swept them away. The divine covenant has a permanence that surpasses the most permanent fixtures that we know:

> *"For the mountains shall depart*
> *And the hills be removed,*
> *But My kindness shall not depart from you.*
> *Nor shall My covenant of peace be removed,"*
> *Says the LORD, who has mercy on you.* (Isa. 54:10)

God's long-term commitment to his people will endure after the mountains themselves are shaken. Israel's present misfortune may be as severe as the flood in many respects, but the covenants are not in jeopardy:

> *For this is like the waters of Noah to me;*
> *For as I have sworn*
> *That the waters of Noah would no longer*
> *   cover the earth,*
> *So have I sworn*
> *That I would not be angry with you,*
> *   nor rebuke you.* (Isa. 54:9)

The dispersion of Israel was a moment of fitful anger, but the covenant is everlasting.

> *For a mere moment I have forsaken you,*
> *But with great mercies I will gather you.*
> *With a little wrath I hid my face from*
> *   you for a moment;*
> *But with everlasting kindness I will have*
> *   mercy on you.* (Isa. 54:7–8)

This great covenant bond is what we become part of in marriage. God honors the marriage covenant and "joins together" husband and wife. The two become one and everything that they have now belongs to the new social unit, that *one*. It is one of the most sheltering experiences of life.

Moreover, God offers to us a relationship that endures beyond life itself. It is based on the "New Covenant": "This cup is the new covenant in my blood," Jesus said. Through the Savior's finished work on the cross, we may enter a relationship with God that is the most permanent, enduring bond we can experience. This steadfast love is everlasting.

Part 5

Shelter and Security

I was in a grand fortress recently on a short holiday trip to Vancouver Island. It was my first visit to Cathedral Grove, but I felt at home instantly. This was one of "my" places, a small acreage of ancient trees, Douglas Fir and Siccus Spruce, just outside Qualicum Beach, British Columbia.

A sign proclaimed one massive fir was "300 years old when Columbus set sail." We stared up its straight trunk, slowly tapering toward the sky, looking for the top. We joined hands and tried to encompass the thing. It would take probably twelve people to encircle this old fellow. We walked among the stately wonders, dwarfed by their immensity and soaked up the soft, mossy greenery and cool dark shades beneath. Oh, if one could design a cathedral with all the qualities of Cathedral Grove—the security of its timelessness, that wonderful sense of awesome stillness, the feeling of being overshadowed—this is what a sanctuary should be.

This kind of shelter is almost the opposite of what I enjoy in a lofty tower. Rather than feeling like the monarch of all I survey, in a forest sanctuary I am dwarfed by the towering figures around me. I feel like an ant, yet I love this feeling as much as the other. Feeling overshadowed by immensities, especially if they are perceived as friendly, somehow puts life in perspective.

This is the surpassing quality of some great shelters. They are so utterly immense, you feel overawed, humbled and reduced. There is no question of bursting through their strength. You are up against something infinitely greater than you are. There is enormous security.

Solidity should be the essence of a good fort, but security also comes to us through the simple, spare shelters we build against the wind and rain. Some of the most fortifying experiences are those we have when a less-than-adequate shelter, such as some abandoned shack, meets a brash, unruly storm. You've ducked inside and are tucked away. You feel the simplicity of shelter and are aware that it does not take much to make a huge difference. There is something special about knowing a deluge is just inches above your head and that it cannot touch you.

Around my parents' little white cottage near Lake Ontario the prevailing wind is from the north. It can blast out of the Northumberland hills with such strength that even a nice sunny day becomes too cool. Better than getting a sweater, though, is to walk down the rickety old steps that lead to the beach. Some twelve feet below the level of the lawns, the beach is always protected. Take a lawn chair or a blanket down there and you can wile away the afternoon with a book while the cool northers sail clear over your head.

Speaking of northers, there were some great winter storms on the outskirts of Montreal during my first pastorate. I vividly remember one stormy night when we were interrupted by a phone call. Some friends from downtown, on their way back from a week-end trip, were stranded on the snow-packed roads. They needed to spend the night with us. Thus, a few friends joined us at a card table, we put a log on the fire, and enjoyed some laughter and warm food and drink. Through the kitchen window, we heard the most outlandish, fiendish wind screaming, blowing in several feet of snow from the north. It was as though we were in an outpost on the fringes of civilization. The warm surprise of that lovely visit lingers as one of the great shelter moments of an icy winter.

I suppose such simple shelters in heavy weather take one back to childhood, where hiding in a boxcar or a culvert during a storm was fairly routine and where the excitement of discovering shelter was most intense! The thing is, you have to be close to the weather to appreciate the shelter. That is the paradox of security: the more aware we are of our own frailty, the more meaningful shelter is to us. Security becomes tangible at those moments when you really know it is there. On the other hand, when we breeze through a day in an air conditioned, climate-controlled environment, we take our securities for granted.

There is a blessed security in having your fort. We savor our security in a fort with very strong walls, yet we also experience security beneath the flimsiest tent. Large or small, immovable or collapsible—these shelters offer the benefit that most of us spend a lifetime pursuing. They provide security.

Chapter 15

Surrounded by Mountains

I like to visit a little restaurant in Canmore, Alberta. It's the setting that appeals to me. Look out any window and you see only gray mass until you look up, way up. Sherwood House is absolutely overshadowed by huge, hovering gray mountains. To me the whole town is a fortress. I walk its streets or hike its riverside trails and sense that I am in a grand fortress surrounded by great walls of granite. I feel the presence of the mountains, almost as though they have drawn close, like a friend. One of my father's poems speaks of mountains that way:

> Hills in the morning that call to come higher,
> Hills at the noontide that challenge and tower;
> Hills like a friend in the even come closer
> Who silent, imparts by his presence his power.[1]

Clearly, this is a whole other side to my grand forts. Here I am among mere mortals, glued to the ground. I am among the people God looks to. "I dwell in the high and holy place," said Isaiah, "with him who has a contrite and humble spirit, to revive the spirit" (Isa. 57:15). When massive things tower above the way Canmari's mountains do, I am overawed. I am reminded of my mortality and relative smallness when I stand at the base of a mass of rock that is older than every building on the continent. Surrounded by mountains close in, especially of the 12,000-foot variety, this fortress makes me feel incredibly secure.

Some people complain of feeling boxed-in in a mountain village with the big, overbearing granite friends looking down all the time. I know some prairie folk who ran back to their flat towns after a year or two of retirement in the more temperate, mountain regions of the country. "Climate isn't everything," they said. "We feel closed-in all the time. Besides those things spoil the view!" I'm sorry for them that they've misunderstood the majesty of the mountains. To me, the mountains convey strong security. They combine immense, mysterious dimensions with an imposing presence. I scarcely visit a mountain hideaway without feeling a special peace.

Mountains also remind me that we have parameters. There are large immovables in our world and we must live somewhere between them. Realizing these parameters is both reassuring and comforting. Our contexts are defined and we can grasp the parameters of our activities. We are not responsible for the state of the universe as a whole, but there is a definite sphere that each of us can affect. When I am in a mountain fortress, I am struck with a sense of my own finiteness. I am not the king of the universe portrayed in a gala exhibition of human achievement; I am a small part of an infinite universe, surrounded by awesome things. I am reduced to a limited sphere and my power to concentrate on that sphere is intensified. Gone is the urge to singlehandedly save the world which in my business can become an overpowering desire almost any day. My limited sphere is more a matter of definition: I am me; I do these things well and with pleasure; I can work within my sphere.

For those of us who tend to get overcommitted, there is a regathering in such settings, especially if you can stay a night or two. The early morning hours in the mountains are the absolute best, but evening shadows also infuse us with rest. For the many middle-aged men I talk to who complain of lacking definition and precision in their work lives, I can prescribe nothing better than a time in the mountains. All the scattered fragments of our own identities, that we have invested and misapplied in a hundred different directions, come together. You feel the imposition of an ordered soul as you stand among mountains.

And a veil of silence settles down. Some explorers of the Cathedral Grove jogged and laughed their way through the ferns beneath the dark presence that towered above us. To me their noise seemed jarring, almost an irreverence. I was hushed and still, like a chastened child. I felt a sense of being overshadowed by immensities, shaded and covered by a huge and stately strength. It was a time to whisper, to be still and recognize deity.

From a distance mountains can be deceiving. They seem so serene on a summer evening when the golden glow of the setting sun casts a warm blanket across their steel-grey flanks. In a mountain town like Canmore, they appear to be benign overseers. Eight-thousand-foot Chinaman's Peak looms overhead. The Three Sisters, rising to 11,000 feet, are just to the east. They are familiar, friendly giants. They seem to welcome you back if you have been away for a time. Pilot Mountain stands at a crossroads along the TransCanada Highway and points the way west as you near Lake Louise. Castle Mountain, shrouded in mist nearby, is like a mysterious old fort you have come to love. Even jagged Mount Rundle has a pleasant side. She stands over Banff like a massive cookie with a very even bite missing from the top. On a summer morning, reflected in the slow-moving Bow River, Rundle is as inviting as a fresh piece of toast by a campfire.

It was on such a morning that we made our decision: we would check out this cookie at close range. A gentle path veered off the service road just west of the Banff Springs Hotel. The Spray River danced and sang through the richly-scented pines. Moss and ferns made the ascent moist and soft under foot. We savored the rich scent of the forest. Someone had leveled the path to make walking easier.

After twenty minutes our pulses had hardly increased. The ascent was so gradual that after forty-five minutes we were surprised to look down and see the Banff hot springs below us. We had made progress! We pressed on undaunted, but the gentle ascent did not continue. By the ninety-minute point we were huffing and puffing and soaked through, and the hot springs were an emerald dot in the river valley below. We were above the tree line and following a precipitous mountain goat trail that went straight up at one point and then disappeared.

At the two-hour mark we stopped dead in our tracks: a fifty-foot wall of granite blocked the way. To reach the summit, we would have to look for another path. We stared at each other and we stared at the massive impasse and gulped down most of our water supply. This mountain resented being scaled.

Veering to the south, we traversed the wide face of Rundle, looking for a break in the cliff that would lead to the summit. Finally we found it: a dry gulch that seemed to cut through the cliff and lead to the peak. We picked our way up the narrow chute, which provided a welcome wall of stone to lean on as we ascended, shedding layers of clothing in the surprisingly hot September sun. Then we were into shale, the sharp, shifting rock that cuts cheap shoes to ribbons and makes upward mobility harder than in the most competitive company on earth. We each had another drop of the precious water. The bottles were almost empty.

With that bit of fresh incentive, tasting the salty sweat that ran off our noses, we pushed for the top. A blister had worked its way up on the top of my toe and was screaming, "No more!" I felt certain the reverse angle going down would be much easier on it.

Majestically, the great cookie itself rose before us with its symmetrical bite. It looked more massive than the very jaws of Melville's Moby Dick. Sure enough, its concave curve seemed very smooth, even up close, as though a nice even set of teeth had taken a huge chomp. But the missing part was not a bite-sized morsel. Traversing the bottom of that gaping, arching bite would take an hour of very careful climbing, if one dared to trek across the thousand feet of steep black walls that fall away precipitously to the huge rocks below.

Four hours after leaving the lush green fields of the Banff springs, we sat on the windy summit. There was no doubt, this baby was no cookie. The mountain had fooled us. It looked inviting, but reaching the summit squeezed out every ounce of energy. Still, the view alone was worth the effort. The sheer northern drop of Rundle is awesome. Lake Minnewanka, where the summer before we had caught trout and the wind can whip up sudden storms that can swamp a small boat, looked like a small azure puddle in the hazy distance—three miles north and one mile down!

You know you are no match for Rundle, even standing at her summit. It is an indomitable mass of wild things, a wilderness of tangled crevasses and impasses. A mountain like that can kill you in a dozen ways: It can dehydrate you. It can put you into a slide of shale that gains momentum as it crashes downward. It can hurtle you off into a void from which there is no return. It can break your limbs and leave you on its impassive face at the mercy of screeching hawks.

How presumptuous we are. We speak of "mountain-moving faith" as though we are dealing with cookies. But mountains are not cookies. Mountains are huge, insurmountable things, the most massive challenge we can face. Mountains are impasses. Mountains are exhaustion. Mountains are mortal danger. They have to do with the wild, uncivilized side of life, when things are out of control. Mountains are obstacles so large they make you feel like a speck alongside them.

Up close or at some distance, mountains speak to me of the strongest immovables of the world. They convey awesome strength, and yet the mountains, great as they are, may someday move. What remains behind them is an even greater, immovable shelter. This is the message of Isaiah.

> *"For the mountains shall depart*
> *And the hills be removed,*
> *But My kindness shall not depart from you.*
> *Nor shall My covenant of peace be removed,"*
> *Says the LORD, who has mercy on you.* (Isa. 54:10)

Who can imagine such a day. Should that happen, what possible refuge would remain? The prophet's assurance is of an even greater shelter—God's lovingkindness will not be removed. His steadfast love must be most unshakable indeed. It must be the most imposing force. Imagine it being directed toward us, surrounding our lives with that kind of enduring presence!

Faith at its best rests on something like mountains. It understands that we are contained in something infinitely greater than ourselves, God's steadfast love. Faith is not so much a matter of holding onto as of being held, for we are held by a love which surpasses our own by as much as a towering mountain surpasses our height. It is something far greater than we are. The greatness is expressed in the words of a classic hymn: "O love, that wilt not let me go, I rest my weary soul in thee. . . ."[2]

The awesome quality of this love is described even more wonderfully by the "much more" passages of Romans 5:

> *For if by the transgression of the one the many died,* much more *did the grace of God . . . abound to the many.* (v. 15 italics added)

God's gift of eternal life far surpasses our offenses, no matter how great they are. His surpassing free gift overflows to all in superabundant grace:

> *If by the transgression of one, death reigned through the one,* much more *those who receive the abundance of grace and of the gift of righteousness will reign in life through the One, Jesus Christ.* (v. 17 italics added)

Death is the great immovable. It hedges humanity about like an unbroken mountain range. The thought of breaking its hold is beyond us, but we are pointed to something greater—life. The power of spiritual life is *much more* than the power of death.

> *Where sin abounded, grace did* much more *abound.* (v. 20 italics added)

The presence of sin is undeniable. But God's compensation for it is so abundant that it *much more* than suffices to counteract sin's influence.

Faith rests in such assurance. It knows that beyond the massive, mountain-like realities of human existence is a loving, forgiving God who will be there when all else has been shaken. Faith sees his love beyond the massive obstacles of this world. It rests in him, regardless of appearances.

Mountains also speak to us of a life of integrity. Simply stated, knowing you have told the truth you can put your mind to rest. Isaiah said, integrity puts you in a mountain stronghold where you are untouchable. Accusations may swirl around you. Misunderstandings may abound. But there is a special protection for the person of integrity.

> *He who walks righteously, and speaks with sincerity,*
> *He who rejects unjust gain,*
> *And shakes his hands so that they hold no bribe;*
> *He who stops his ears from hearing about bloodshed,*
> *And shuts his eyes from looking upon evil;*
> *He will dwell on the heights;*
> *His refuge will be the impregnable rock;*
> *His bread will be given him;*
> *His water will be sure.* (Isa. 33:15–16)

There is something about integrity that surrounds a life with enormous, sheltering strength.

Our lives can be lived in such a way that enormous security surrounds them. All of the uncertainties and fears are kept out of this sheltered place. There is a great bulwark of strength round about. This security has to do with faith in God's unfailing love. When we go beyond mental assent and really rest on the assurance of a love that is stronger than mountains, we enjoy a level of security that is unmatched.

In trying to define faith as "resting with assurance," I used an object lesson. "You didn't test the pews this morning, did you?" I asked the congregation. "I was watching you and you did not test them. You just sat down. In fact, some of you just 'plunked' down and put up your 'Do Not Disturb' signs. Why would you be so trusting?" The audience looked at me as though their worst fears about the pastor had finally come to pass.

"Have you been under those pews lately?" I continued. "Well I have. I was down there"—this was for the benefit of all those who believe ministers do not know which end of the screwdriver to hold—"with the Men's Fellowship members reinforcing those pews. I happen to know they are not as strong as you think. You really should check them out before you sit down." I described the iron bars we had screwed across the bottoms of some of these padded pews to keep them from breaking apart. "You people just sit down because you trust Canadian craftsmanship, for whatever reason."

That, I said, is what faith is. We are put right with God through the death of his Son and he asks us to *lean* on that in the way we sing about in the great hymn:

> That soul that on Jesus has leaned for repose
> I will not, I will not desert to its foes;
> That soul though all hell should endeavour to shake,
> I'll never, no never, no never forsake.[3]

Understanding faith in this way takes us out of the realm of personal initiative, where my eternal salvation is dependent on the strength of my spiritual forearms, to the finished work of Christ himself. I stake all my destiny on him.

"You would demonstrate faith best," I said, "if you lay right out on those pews. You would show how much you trust them, by putting *all* your weight on them." And putting all our weight on Christ's finished work imparts security which goes beyond the greatest life can offer. It is a security that transcends time. Putting our full weight on him allows us to be held in something much greater than ourselves, the eternal love of the Almighty.

There is one other aspect of the shelter of the mountains, one that is vitally important. The parameters that reduce our perceptions of ourselves to a more limited sphere, the integrity and regathering imposed by the awesome silence, the security of knowing we are held tightly and securely by God's immovable everlasting love turns our attention to our own lifestyles. When our words and deeds are characterized by righteousness, sincerity, and justice, we "dwell on the heights." When we avoid moral compromise, our "refuge" is the "impregnable rock." When we trust Christ fully for salvation, his righteousness is bestowed upon us. The confidence with which we live has to do with his life being lived through us. Our lives are hidden with Christ in God.

Chapter 16

Enlarge the Place
of Your Tent

A tent is a spare and basic fort, one that would seem to be flimsy
and able to provide only a modicum of shelter. But, when viewed
with the proper perspective, a tent becomes a strong, secure forti-
fication. Last summer, on the far side of Vancouver Island, a tent
housed our family. It was not a strong tent, just the basic pup, the
kind used by novices who camp reluctantly once in a long while.
But, for a few fitful nights at least, the little thing did the job. It
kept out the fine rain that moved in off the Pacific and thoroughly
soaked the shoreline. As long as the wind stayed down, which was
not often the case, our little shelter was quite cozy. And, goodness,
the sound of raindrops tapping on the canvas while we were dry
and warm inside made for the best kind of shelter.

The breakers of the Pacific are huge, strong, and loud. It takes a
night or two for them to become a lullaby. When you thrust your
head out in the morning and look on the awakening world, you feel
like Noah. There is the joyous promise of discovery, of a world
refurbished while you slept. You have instant physical contact with
the wondrous world of sand and sea: a wide beach strewn with the
busy morning world of little creatures, long strings of seaweed you
might like to wind around a Christmas tree, starfish, the abandoned shells of crabs that have forsaken their crusty shelters for a
hole in the sand, sea breezes that beat on your face.

How different this contact, this instant engagement with the environment, from the lengthy process of emergence that most of us go through most days in the working year. We are so removed from the elements, we feel impervious to them. We assume that we can avoid the weather any time we want. We forget both how chilling exposure can be and how great it is to be covered.

How is it possible that we could experience secure shelter in this frail covering? It is because our greatest experience of shelter occurs when we are closest to the storm.

In defining *simplicity,* Richard Foster stresses unity of heart and singleness of purpose. He says, "We have only one desire: to obey Christ in all things. We have only one purpose: to glorify Christ in all things."[1] I recognize that kind of unity when I am in some of my simple shelters. There just isn't room for a thousand collector's items or electronic distractions. Shelter itself is the primary thing, especially if outside the storm is intense. Life is reduced to the barest essentials. After all, you will have to put everything on your back and trek it out.

Another quality of simplicity is *joy in God's good creation.* I associate some of my best frail shelters with this closeness to nature. Without the wind and rain, physical shelter is less meaningful. And the closer you are to feeling the elements on your face, the more precious the shelter becomes.

We all thought it strange when Darlene moved back to Jamaica. She had a good Canadian home, a job, excellent schools for her children. "But life here is too clean," she said, "too tidy. Everything is in plastic, concrete, and glass. I miss Jamaica." Her bright eyes widened as she spoke of her land: The casual contact with neighbors out the back door or the front; the pervasive disorder of society that enhances opportunities for serendipities and community life. I think she touched on our antiseptic, private culture that too often is insensitive and lonely. In her eyes, our technological advances have made it difficult for us to live simply and fully.

In providing handles for simplicity, Richard Foster says, "Get in touch with the earth. Revel in the infinite variety of colors around you. . . . Enjoy the texture of grass and leaves."[2] Our large, modern cities make this difficult. At least for Darlene, it was im-

possible. And her appetite for the earth, for simplicity, was strong
enough that to her a considerable sacrifice was acceptable.

Even though your shelter is sparse, there are qualities that im-
part security. One thing is that you don't want to leave. Just as a
mountain fortress had me so hooked that it felt like pulling up
garden beets when I returned to city life, some of these sparse
shelters keep you hanging on. Their spiritual qualities give them
strength. The unity of heart and closeness to the earth produce a
growth of the spirit that is very strong. You feel like Thoreau in his
rustic cabin at Walden Pond:

> By poverty, i.e. simplicity of life and fewness of incidents, I am
> solidified and crystallized, as a vapor or liquid by cold. It is a
> singular concentration of strength and energy and flavor. . . .
> You think that I am impoverishing myself by withdrawing from
> men, but in my solitude I have woven for myself a silken web or
> chrysalis, and, nymph-like, shall ere long burst forth a more
> perfect creature, fitted for a higher society. By simplicity . . .
> my life is concentrated and so becomes organized, or a cosmos,
> which before was inorganic and lumpish.[3]

Perhaps it is for such reasons that you can derive a sense of permanence from frail shelters, a sense of lasting spiritual security.
Isaiah often speaks of tents in these strong, stable terms:

> *Enlarge the place of your tent;*
> *Stretch out the curtains of your dwellings,*
>   *spare not;*
> *Lengthen your cords,*
> *Strengthen your pegs.*
> *For you will spread abroad to the right*
>   *and to the left.* (Isa. 54:2–3 NASV)

A strong tent is a symbol of divine favor. The nation, like a
desolate woman, would soon bear many sons who would possess
nations and resettle the desolate cities (see Isa. 54:3). Former days
of shame and reproach would be forgotten. Permanence and stability would return to national life. A restored Jerusalem is compared

to a tent "which shall not be folded, its stakes shall never be pulled up, nor any of its cords be torn apart" (Isa. 33:20 NASV). This is an act of God toward people who "wait" upon him: "Be Thou their strength every morning, our salvation also in time of distress (Isa. 33:2 NASV).

This is the singleness of vision that often accompanies a spare shelter. Though we are surrounded by the most meager walls, we have a strong sense of security because we are spiritually whole.

> *He shall be the stability of your times,*
> *A wealth of salvation, wisdom and knowledge;*
> *The fear of the LORD is his treasure* (Isa. 33:6 NASV).

Chapter 17

A House Not Made with Hands

An ancient king got the worst news: his death was imminent. Then the sentence was revoked and fifteen years were added to his life. Through the turmoil of those days, he had time to reflect deeply about life. Life, he said, is like a tent: "Like a shepherd's tent my dwelling is pulled up and removed from me; as a weaver I rolled up my life" (Isa. 38:12). Now that sounds more like the tents I know: collapsible. And it is a theme that is picked up in the New Testament by Paul: "For we know that if the earthly tent which is our house is torn down, we have a building from God, a house not made with hands, eternal in the heavens" (2 Cor. 5:1).

To my mind, nothing could more strongly convey our lack of permanence in this life. Our bodies are certainly not made to be immortal. Indeed it is a wonder we last as long as we do! The images from both Isaiah and Paul remind us that there is no ultimate security in this life. All of our lives are "pulled up and removed" like a shepherd's tent. We should live in ways that acknowledge that.

Strangely enough, we receive strong inner security in inverse proportion to our physical securities. When we protect our lot as though we were building castles for eternity, we shrivel up and move off the scene in a hurry. But when we accept life as a *pilgrim-*

age, enormous security is built in along the way. This is the "modesty and temperance in all things" that we associate with simplicity. "Our lives are marked by voluntary abstinence in the midst of extravagant luxury."[1]

Voluntary or not—some of us are dragged off on camping trips, you know—the simplicity and frailty of some of my forts give a sense of oneness with the poor and simple people of the world. A camping holiday is a reminder of how basic, how elemental, shelter is. It's strange how many of us leave our comfortable homes in suburbia to trek off to the wilds to live in tents for our holidays. We choose to identify with simplicity for a time.

For the very poor, a sheet of canvas against the elements is an enormous luxury, and a flapping tent gives you a certain sense of identity with them. Richard Foster says, "Simplicity takes outward shape through conscious identification with the poor and forgotten. Jesus Christ did so repeatedly and so must we. The exact expression of our identification will have infinite variety, but there is no doubt that we ought to engage in this loving work."[2]

It's hard to picture Jesus among the transients, with no home, no security, no long-term support. And yet he seemed to identify with them when he said to an eager scribe, "Foxes have holes and birds of the air have nests, but the Son of Man has nowhere to lay His head" (Matt. 8:20). *You can identify with my teaching,* he seems to say, and the scribe's enthusiastic response left little doubt about that. *But what about my lifestyle?* Jesus asked. *Do you really want to follow me?*

It wasn't entirely true, when you think of it, that *Jesus had no bed.* There was, after all, his home in Nazareth where it seems he enjoyed close to thirty years in a loving environment. Early glimpses suggest it was a place of responsibility and acceptance. Yet, when the decisive moment arrived, he chose to live without a home. Certainly, he had a desire to identify publicly with the religious fervor surrounding John the Baptist. When Jesus left Nazareth and went down to the Jordan to be baptized, a unique sense of calling dawned. It was time to sever the ties with his home base. "Who is my mother and who are my brothers?" he asked later. "I am he that does the will of God," he said (see Mark 3:33–35). He accepted the hospitality of Peter, his friends at Bethany and a variety of strangers. He slept in the back of a boat. No doubt he often lay down under the stars like the Old Testament Jacob did. The one who was born out behind the inn lived that way in life. By choice he had no place to lay his head.

It was a fitting choice. In the largest sense, Jesus left his home when he "made himself of no reputation and took upon himself the form of a servant and was made in the likeness of man" (Phil. 2). He identified completely with our human weaknesses when he fully became man. It was fitting that he experience homelessness in every dimension. Some of our best-loved hymns dwell upon the homeless one who left the Father's "house of light":

> Out of the ivory palaces, into a world of woe,
> Only his great, eternal love made my Saviour go.[3]

> Thou didst leave Thy throne
> And Thy kingly crown,
> When Thou camest to earth for me;
> But in Bethlehem's home
> Was there found no room
> For Thy holy nativity.
> O come to my heart, Lord Jesus,
> There is room in my heart for Thee.[4]

Those who love Christ want to offer him a resting place in the heart. And, according to Revelation 3:20, that is what he seeks. "Behold I stand at the door and knock. If anyone hears my voice and opens the door, I will come in to him and dine with him, and he with Me." This is the lowly, humble Christ, patiently looking for an open door where he can "sup." We like to repeat the words of the disciples who were walking with Christ on the road to Emmaus. They said, "Abide with us." And the hymn says:

> Abide with me:
> fast falls the eventide;
> The darkness deepens;
> Lord with me abide.[5]

The only fitting response to the homeless Christ is just that kind of invitation. *Lord, make my life your resting place.*

In a broader sense, Jesus' statement, nowhere to lay my head, describes *the church*. His comment was addressed to a would-be follower, but it implies something about all followers of Christ: We need to identify with Christ's homelessness as well as his teaching.

Some say the church is at its best when *it* has nowhere to lay its head. When it is a restless, seeking force in the world, pained by the plight of the homeless around it, always seeking and saving that which is lost—*then* it seems to identify most with its Lord. Dietrich Bonhoeffer put it most eloquently:

> The Church is her true self only when she exists for humanity. As a fresh start she should give away all her endowments to the poor and needy. The clergy should live solely on the free-will offerings of their congregations, or possibly engage in some secular calling. She must take her part in the social life of the world, not lording it over men, but helping and serving them. She must tell men, whatever their calling, what it means to live in Christ, to exist for others.[6]

When the church eschews its own security, its comforts, the solidity of its institutions and buildings, and follows its Lord out into the streets and marketplaces of this world—that is when it is truest to its calling. It follows. If Jesus had no place to lay his head, why should his Body recline in comfortable pews? The Body must extend the incarnation. We are called to participate in the suffering and weariness of our Lord. Paul states the truth in its ultimate form: "Always bearing about in the body the dying of Jesus, that the life also of Jesus may be manifest in our bodies" (2 Cor. 4:10). Unless we can identify with Jesus' dying, we will hardly be identified with his life.

Of course, the implications of Christ's homelessness can be pretty devastating for the comfortable, middle-class Christianity that has emerged in this society. It's like living our comfortable lives and trying to relate to the homeless. Isn't there a fundamental incompatibility between my heated waterbed and the homeless

Christ? One can't help but wonder how comfortable Jesus would be in some of our homes. Perhaps his challenge is not so much to a cultic freedom from houses and property as to a fundamental detachment from the ease and materialism of the times.

I hear a challenge to awareness of the transients of my own community who populate psychiatric hospitals and correctional institutions or just live on the streets. These ones need to feel the presence, through the Church, of a Christ who seeks them with a restless, unstinting love.

"Where do you dwell?" ask some early followers of Jesus. He replies, "Come and see." It is as though he has no fixed address, like "Mary," whose story was told in our newspaper.

> She sleeps on the grass near to the city hall. Recently, all her identification was stolen from her purse which she had stowed under her head for safe-keeping. She is adamant that, at 55, she wants to work, but with no papers, and no fixed address, how many employers will hire?[7]

Just follow me, says the Jesus of no fixed address, in the free, adventurous lifestyle I have chosen. That is all you need. Perhaps he says that to all of us, when we are too prone to identify his kingdom with sites and buildings. He is the mobile Christ. To "come and see" where he dwells is a lifetime's adventure in moving.

Lisa and Mike Sharkey have two kids and a house in my neighborhood. Actually the house is more of a stop-over place. It's often filled with the street people they bring home. "Home" for this couple is really the streets downtown. He was raised there. Now he operates a ministry to prostitutes called "Bridging the Gap" where street kids can find a different pursuit: the passion of the New Testament church; the seeking spirit of Christ that identifies with them in their utter exposure and homelessness.

"No place to lay his head." The phrase describes the Lord and, by implication, his followers. Then, the phrase seems to do one more thing: In a sense, it describes the true *state of all mankind*. Perhaps in this "Son of Man" statement, Jesus is saying something about representative man, federal man, the true man. It's true of us all. We really have no resting place on this earth.

That is hard to believe when we're surrounded by family and friends and the wonderful sense of security that we are able to derive from familiar things. Essentially homeless on earth—how can that be? Yet it's something we've known about all along even though we've pretended differently. This unexpressed knowledge is described in some of our best songs and poems in the way parts have of expressing for us our true feelings:

> I'm just a poor, wayfarin' stranger
> While travelin' through this world of woe,
> There is no sickness, toil or danger
> In that fair land to which I go.[8]

> The woods are lovely, dark and deep
> But I have promises to keep
> And miles to go before I sleep
> And miles to go before I sleep.[9]

> A noiseless patient spider,
> I mark'd where on a little promontory it stood isolated,
> Mark'd how to explore the vacant vast surrounding,
> It launch'd forth filament, filament, filament, out of itself,
> Ever unreeling them ever tirelessly speeding them.

> And you O my soul where you stand,
> Surrounded, detached, in measureless oceans of space,
> Ceaseless musing, venturing, throwing, seeking the spheres
>   to connect them
> Till the bridge you will need be form'd, till the ductile
>   anchor hold,
> Till the gossamer thread you fling catch somewhere,
>   O my soul.[10]

Yes, our souls are built on eternal dimensions and we cannot truly settle down and rest in this mortal life. How can you lay your head here, we might ask, when you were designed to rest it on the bosom of Abraham? Jesus said, "In my Father's house are many mansions. . . . I go to prepare a place for you." The apostle Paul looks forward to a time when "this tent" of our earthly body is "torn down" to be replaced with a more permanent dwelling, "a building from God, a house not made with hands, eternal in the heavens" (2 Cor. 5:1).

We are called to be followers of the one who had no place to lay his head. It follows that we should not lay down our own heads too comfortably on this mortal clay. Really, the only rest we have is in Christ. "Come unto me," he says, "all ye that labor and are heavy laden, and I will give you rest."

And in that rest, let us now lay down our heads in careless indifference. Rather than *lay down,* let us *lift up:* "lift up your eyes and look at the fields, for they are already white for harvest" (John 4:35). Again, "lift up your heads, because your redemption draws near" (Luke 21:28).

Part 6

Shelter as Structure

Some of my childhood forts were built in the midst of tumult. Ballgames, fistfights, marbles and cards, cowboys and Indians, piano lessons, girls, hockey, hooky, and pranks—bringing order out of the chaos of those days must have been something on the scale of creation itself. But left to myself, I would build an orderly fort with strong walls of solid ice, front and top entrances, an array of missiles for prompt defense. How is it that those grimy ten-year-old hands produced such order? I had purpose.

These days, a lunch hour retreat fills much the same function. It brings order out of chaos. It imposes structure on a week that may have come unravelled. I tap into purpose, to an overall meaning and design.

Neil O'Shea died suddenly on the job at fifty-four. He was a natural designer, taking his skills to the city hall planning department early in his career and rising to the top with very little formal training. His fellow planners were out in force at his funeral.

"God is the master designer," I said. "He brought order out of chaos. He separated the light from the darkness, the water from the land. Order and symmetry and design—these things are vital to him." He made us in his image to be designers in the world, to replenish the earth, to cultivate and keep the garden. He must be very close, I reasoned, to designers by profession. Then I asked those folk at the graveside to consider that at that moment we were part of God's great design for our lives. It was difficult to see, of course, considering the tragedy that brought us there, but "God causes all things to work together for good to those who love God, to those who are called according to His purpose" (Rom. 8:28).

Such things do not become clear at gravesides. It takes time to see the structure of our lives, the design that integrates things. It takes time, and perhaps a fort.

Chapter 18

_____

Like a Walled River

"**P**eace like a river" seemed a long way from the reality of one summer's canoe trip. Jeff and I slipped the seventeen-foot canoe into the waters of the Bow River. Between Lake Louise and Banff is a choice stretch of rapid water, especially in the early summer when the river turns emerald green from the spring run-off in the mountains. There is a good deal of white water to crash through, and the paddling is effortless. For the most part, it is more a matter of staying in the swelling current and avoiding rocks than of propelling the craft forward. A deft "J" stroke is your best contribution while you are being swept along by the rush of icy mountain water pushing toward the sea.

Our day was wild. We were caught in a brief storm around noon that drove us off the water into the trees. We shivered beneath the overturned canoe, which we had leaned against a poplar tree while we fumbled around in our knapsacks for a change of clothes. Back in the water after the storm passed, we had a scary moment when a large rock caught us midship and the canoe began to turn sideways. We had avoided it at the nose, but the rear of the craft had not swung wide enough. Fortunately, we sprang loose before capsizing, but it was a close call. It made me wonder what we were doing out there. And of course, at the end of the day our shoulders ached and our joints were stiff. We had all the cramps and weather-beaten weariness of landlubbers after a day on the water.

But there was also a very sheltered moment just toward the end of the day. We were out of the rapid water and dusk was settling in. We hardly had the strength to paddle another stroke. We floated into a wide, still stretch of river whose waters looked black in the shadows. The receding shades of pink behind us threw a glow on the Sawtooth mountain range on the left. The dark woods marked our course on either side. The river had become absolutely still, reflecting the black trees at the side and the deepening shades of the sky. The silence was broken only by the twittering of frogs and insects. The crack of a beaver's tail issued a sharp warning to his colony. We saw him cutting across the river, forming a "V" on the water with his nose amid the circles of jumping trout.

We were aware of peace—the peace of effortless, gentle progress after an exhausting day. It was the peace of circumscribed course. It was the spellbinding peace of nature's beauty under the glorious setting sun.

For Isaiah the difference between a river and the sea is this matter of peace. He said, "Your peace would have been like a river" (Isa. 48:18), but "the wicked are like the troubled sea, when it cannot rest, whose waters cast up mire and dirt. . . . There is no peace . . . for the wicked" (Isa. 57:20–21).

You can have a life that is constrained by walls, that does not flow at random over the countryside. You can have a life that is not tossed by wide-ranging storms that constantly churn up water. It has a prescribed course. It flows from the Bow Glacier to the South Saskatchewan River and then to Lake Winnipeg and Hudson Bay. The water moves. Even when it widens out and meanders, its destiny is never in doubt. This, said Isaiah, is the life to aspire to. It is simple. It has walls. It has few choices. The assignment is to follow a prescribed course.

Or you can have a lifestyle that is so restless and troubled it is like an ocean. It has no constraints. It is one wave of troubled restlessness after another. It is a life of continual upheaval.

The difference between a peaceful river and the turbulent sea also has to do with flow. One is going somewhere; the other is not. The life like a river has walls; the life like the sea does not. These are the factors that give a river the image of peace for Isaiah, and liken the sea to unrest.

Flow is essential to a peaceful life. Your goals should flow into each other. There is something about forward movement—progress—that infuses a life with peace. Lose that sense of flow and life becomes troubled like a restless sea, casting up unsavory things.

Richard Leider's book *The Power of Purpose* is one of the best discussions I have found about retaining goals and flow in life. He says you should write a statement of purpose and paste it on your bathroom mirror or some other place that is highly visible:

> Every one of us needs a reason to get up in the morning. What's yours? If you're waiting for a great leader or organization to create . . . purpose in your life—you might wait your whole life long.[1]

How do you direct your restless energies that heave and thrash like the sea? How do you give your life flow so that your goals merge and there is a sense of progression about what you do? Leider suggests reflecting on your favorite pastimes. We discover life's great purpose by understanding what we already like to do.

I periodically give myself a quiz to help define my life's purpose: List seven events in a day you were a part of that you enjoyed. The examples do not need to be dramatic. On seven three by five cards write a paragraph describing each experience. Arrange the cards in order of the importance of the experiences. On each card circle one word that sums up the experience. Using the same key words, write a statement about yourself.

Before long you have a purpose statement for your life that comes directly from the things you already enjoy doing. Once you have purpose, walls encase your life. It is easier to say no to invitations, sales pitches, job offers, that aren't right for you. And saying no is one of the key ingredients to staying on course.

When Isaiah spoke to his people about peaceful rivers and tossing seas, he was teaching them about moral and immoral lifestyles. The nation was oppressed and in captivity. They could readily understand a peace that flows like a river and that it is the result of obedience. But they could only acknowledge Isaiah's truth in hindsight for the nation had been characterized by disobedience: "You were obstinate, and your neck was an iron sinew, and your brow bronze" (Isa. 48:4). As a result, all semblance of peace was gone from national life. The river image brought forth a sigh—if only you had been obedient your peace would be like a river. Instead you have been "tested in the furnace of affliction" (see Isa. 48:10).

> *Inasmuch as these people have rejected the gently*
>   *flowing rivers of Shiloah,*
> *And rejoice in Resin . . .*
> *Now therefore, behold, the Lord is about to bring*
>   *on them the strong and abundant waters*
>   *of the Euphrates,*
> *Even the king of Assyria and all his glory;*
> *And it will rise up over all its channels and go*
>   *over all its banks.*
> *Then it will sweep on into Judah, it will overflow*
>   *and pass through,*
> *It will reach even to the neck.* (Isa. 8:6–8)

Another passage about peaceful rivers reminds us of the virtues of simplicity. All the people had to do was follow instructions. They needed to obey just as Foster reminds us that "we have only one purpose: to obey Christ in all things." Obedience creates structure; structure creates simplicity.

Simplicity creates a profound sense of shelter. Life has been scaled down. Interests have been reduced. There is a peaceful, river-like flow. One notices this sense of peace in people who are on a week-end retreat. They have united with friends in a common theme for a few days. There is a peaceful process in their lives. Some of the seniors I know are close to this kind of peace. For many of them life has scaled down to the essentials, and there is an even flow and pace to their days. Many of the rest of us are busy living one day at a time, making money and being enterprising—

complicating our lives but giving little thought to the future. Too much works against contentment.

Our home has fairly frequent divisions over the issue of simplicity versus entrepreneurial tendencies and I am the culprit. I like to have a number of projects under way. Writing, building, buying and selling, refinishing, installing, redecorating, trading—I get a sense of life from this kind of action. Seeing something happening out there, some investment going on, helps me feel good. I get restless when I am restricted to doing my job and exercising my gifts on the simplest level. I like to complicate the process.

Ruth, on the other hand, likes a simple, well-tailored process. No debts, no risks, no new outlay of money until everything already bought is paid for—that is her ideal. If only I could relax and enjoy such a world. And we have it that way from time to time, but it seems we savor it only for a little while and then I throw a new project in the machinery to further challenge our resources.

How long does it take someone like me to heed the Scripture's call to contentment and simplicity of purpose? We need to focus more on our own gifts. The violinist who is moving toward concert status, for example, has little time for entrepreneurial projects. This is the challenge I see confronting me. Simplifying our lives enables us to achieve greatness on one or two fronts, leaving the pursuit of wealth and other things to others.

Those who live simple lives are, as Matthew Arnold wrote, "Bounded by themselves and unregardful in what state God's other works may be."[2] We enjoy the greatest sense of peace when we function within a constraining purpose. A bright, strong goal casts a certain spell over our lives that keeps us functioning smoothly. Once there's purpose, there's a flow; the river of life doesn't meander all over the countryside. We have the power to stay on course. All the troubling, debilitating indecisions get left behind in the laughing rush of purpose.

The walls that bring peace to our lives are constructed by a guiding purpose. Difficulties arise when we build the walls before we discover our purposes. My friend Ron leads his household by this principle. If a son says he is not sure what he would like to do,

Ron says, "Let me decide for you," and he enrolls the boy in a trade. In helping his sons establish their purposes, he has produced an electrician and a plumber and is grooming a carpenter. They each have a trade and later, he says, they can do what they want. Smart father.

Don, on the other hand, chose a trade without much thought about his purpose and found only frustration. Just after high school, he enrolled in the electrical trade. His enjoyment of math had always been minimal, and he found himself facing a great deal of math. But art and music were his true loves. He was truly unhappy. The walls of his trade constrained him before his purpose was really clear to him. A painful process of a misdirected effort and conflict eventually freed him to enroll in the College of Art and play in a band. The financial prospects of his redirected purpose are not promising, but he has renewed enthusiasm for life and now his life has structure.

However it is arrived at purpose can contribute enormous stability. And the stability gives you a strong sense of shelter. Your life flows within its walls, and you have peace like a river.

Chapter 19

City Walls

If anything, our town is overly regulated. Street-lights, stop signs, traffic signals—everything is done to excess. When in doubt, the traffic people seem to say, add a stop sign. It all makes the city's favorite phrase, *rapid transit,* a bit of a conundrum.

The worst offender is "the island." Inserted down the middle of virtually every street of any size, the island makes left turns impossible. Coming out of the shopping center or gas station, you have to turn right—we *always* turn right in our town—and then look for a chance to make a U-turn.

At first I was quite frustrated with this concern for regulation. I had thought that any town with the nickname "Cowtown" would have pretty easygoing attitudes toward traffic. After I picked up my fortieth parking ticket, however, I began to see the "light," and the signs too!

This is a law-and-order town. It has to do with pioneer days. One of the first settlers described his arrival and the feeling of pride that persists among our residents still:

Never will I forget the sight that met our eyes—the confluence of the two winding rivers with their wooded banks, the verdant valley, and beyond the wide expanse of green plain that stretched itself in homage to the distant blue mountains. After the barren march of 1874 through the barren lands of the south, after the hard winter in Fort Macleod and the wide, bare prairies of the early part of this trip, that at last we had received our reward, that this was the "Promised Land." A wonderful country! A Garden of Eden! A place to live forever! My home ever since.[1]

Surrounded by vast prairie, the Northwest Mounted Police established a fort here in 1875. Immediately there were rumors of trouble on the North Saskatchewan River involving one Gabriel Dumont, a buffalo hunter who wanted an independent state. Then the fort itself was brought close to mutiny when the commander decided to name it after himself, "Fort Brisbois." It took the intervention of the national Minister of Justice to defuse the situation. He named the new fort Fort Calgary, after a Gaelic word meaning "clear running water."

The little fort imposed its structure upon the wilds early on. A large barracks and a guardroom for twelve prisoners were built. There were stables, a blacksmith shop, and a hospital with eight beds. Each day at ten hundred hours there was a mounted parade complete with inspection. Twice a week there was a full dress parade. By 1885 the fort had been upgraded to District Headquarters and had a full-time police officer for a burgeoning town of 500. His job description was "to arrest all drunken and disorderly people; to stop all fast driving and racing in the town; and to attend all fires." *Wanted* posters advertised the pursuit of all kinds of unsavory characters: horse thieves, who could receive a sentence of as much as twenty years in jail, robbers, who held up stagecoaches on the Edmonton-Calgary run, and other outlaws who in general made life dangerous. Saturday nights presented unique problems such as, "More than one enthusiastic patron charged his horse right up the steps of the Alberta Hotel and reined in at the 'longest bar in the west.'"[2]

And there was always unrest outside the walls of the fort. By the middle of 1885, the Northwest Rebellion scare was in full swing. Every night the town was filled with reports of uprisings among the neighboring Indians. The powerful Blackfoot tribe lived just to the east of Calgary, and the Sarcees were a menace to the west.

The men of the fort became accustomed to banding together to go out and quell unrest beyond the walls.

So, our young city which today is home to three-quarters of a million people, is really a fort. It was established to impose order on an unruly land, a vast stretch of prairie the national government was trying to assimilate. Eventually the city subdued the wilderness and established order, even if sometimes I don't like it.

Ancient Judah looked to its cities for the imposition of order too, and Isaiah contrasted the unruly wilderness with the civilized city. He said there would be a time of desolation and a time of restoration.

Beat your breasts for the pleasant fields, for the fruitful vine,
For the land of my people in which thorns and briars shall
    come up;
Yea, for all the joyful houses, and for the jubilant city.
Because the palace has been abandoned, the populated
    city forsaken.
Hill and watch-tower have become caves forever,
A delight for wild donkeys, a pasture for flocks.

Until the Spirit is poured out upon us from on high,
And the wilderness becomes a fertile field . . .
Then my people will live in a peaceful habitation,
And in secure dwellings and in undisturbed resting
    places. (Isa. 32:12–18 NASV)

He also warned the people that they must live obediently with God's purposes always in their minds. If they didn't they would fall into sin and their cities would be destroyed. "And this will be the full price of the pardoning of his sin. . . . The fortified city is isolated, a homestead forlorn and forsaken like the desert" (Isa. 27:9–10 NASV).

Tyre had been a place of merchandise and mirth. It was to be broken down and emptied (see Isa. 24:2, 8, 10). Damascus was about to be "removed from being a city" and would become a "fallen ruin" (see Isa. 17:1). They were proud cities, but they were filled with sin. Under divine judgment they were turned into dwellings for owls. And according to Isaiah's prophecy, Babylon "will never be inhabited or lived in from generation to generation" (Isa. 13:20 NASV).

Historians say Babylon was one of the first cities created on the scale of a modern metropolis. It was one of the first places on earth to experience the disadvantages and advantages of crowded city life. It was laid out about 2000 B.C. in the shape of a rectangle, with all the buildings arranged in a geometrical pattern. The streets were straight and of uniform width. Walls intersected at right angles. Private houses, complete with inner courtyards, were miniature versions of the temples and palaces. But it was destroyed and Isaiah praised God for the destruction. "O Lord . . . I will exalt Thee," he said, "for Thou has made a city into a heap, a fortified city into a ruin" (Isa. 25:1-2). This is the lesson for us: A people who live in sin have their cities destroyed, but the people who trust God will be sheltered in a strong, secure city:

> *We have a strong city;*
> *He sets up walls and ramparts for security.*
> *Open the gates that the righteous nation might enter,*
> *The one that remains faithful.* (Isa. 26:1-2)

I look around the city of three-quarter million people that Calgary has become and wonder about its early days. The modern city is such a jungle during rush hour, for example, it is hard for us to relate to a need to impose order on a wilderness or to develop a community, security, entertainment. Still, having dwelt in cities all my life, I am always conscious of the hum of a huge network of life all around, of lights and warmth and order, of the shelter provided me by my city.

One of my favorite paintings shows children in a playground surrounded by their town. You recognize the shelter of the community when you imagine the scene without the buildings. A playground in the middle of a prairie would give a sense of tremendous freedom, but it couldn't convey the carefree security of a playground protected by a surrounding city.

These qualities of the city are in jeopardy today, and with them a good deal of our sense of shelter. To lose *community,* to lose the *rule of law,* is to expose ourselves to something worse than the original wilderness. We must strengthen our commitment to these fine forts.

And a well-kept house and yard contribute much shelter, both to its inhabitants and to its town. To preserve such things is to take a stand against the growing desolation of the times.

Chapter 20

Foundations and Roots

The engine of technology is racing along with knowledge as its fuel. The pace of change has become intolerable. The permanence that we once associated with homes has been swept away. People, things, places, organizations, ideas—none have the permanence we need. Every new discovery, every technological advance, seems to increase our transience and distance from old values and roots. We face so much novelty as the old order crumbles around us we never "feel at home." Cloning, computers, laser holographs and other areas of incessant technological breakthrough create in us a growing weariness and wariness with change. We live with diversity and fragmentation on a level unmatched in the history of mankind.

We face so much potential for overchoice that many of us experience a kind of adaptive breakdown and paralysis. Is it possible that the resilience of the human race is being pushed to the limits? Are we tampering with the biological stability of mankind? These are the questions Toffler raises as he calls for, among other things, new roots.[1] We always need foundations.

The fence at the rear of my yard leans fearfully outward. To passing joggers on the green belt behind, it might even appear threatening. Its angle of tilt is well beyond that of Pisa's leaning tower. But, I explain to the property manager, one does not just rush out and fix the back fence. It's on my "to do" list, but the back fence is at the back of the pack. And I am not working my way back awfully fast. There are a lot of "front-row customers" calling for attention. The fence may just have to lean a while longer.

The fence problem is a matter of foundations, of course. My neighbor did nothing to enhance my fence's appearance when he dug down and laid a grand foundation for the one at the back of his yard. New cedar posts set in concrete, a superb, rigidly straight new fence—it makes the angle on mine look all the more acute. Before he called in the experts, his fence and mine leaned out there together like two old companions of many a western gale. The passersby might well have needed to check twice to see if our angle was vertical or not. Now there is no doubt. It is quite clear someone's fence is badly out of whack and there is no doubt whose it is. Mine needs a new foundation.

We had a church building in our town that was dropping an inch or two a year, or so they said. It is now a parking lot and rightfully so. The foundation was weak. It had been built on fill.

Our present facility, on the other hand, is built on solid bedrock. It sits on an abutment of the Rocky Mountains known as Nose Hill, a mass of bedrock along the north of the city. So impervious is the rock, the design of the church had to be revised. Now, rather than having Christian Education facilities below, they sit up on top like a penthouse suite. There is nothing like a bit of bedrock to force innovation. Some visitors like the idea enough to take it home on paper.

They tell me that our downtown office towers have foundations that go down almost as far below the ground as the skyscrapers ascend above. The mix of concrete and steel is so firm a huge tower can rise eighty-five floors into the windy western sky, solid as a rock.

Thinking of firm foundations, I have a friend, B. J., who has not moved from Ottawa since the day of his birth. I remember attending church with him and Kids' Club and summer camps. And I remember other things. One summer we biked twenty miles out to his family's summer place, Lett's Rest, and got hopelessly sunburned. His grandmother coated my skin with the cure best known in those days, one which mercifully has not been heard of since—potato peels. I lay on the hammock semi-delirious, covered in a great blanket of potato peels, and reflected on the meaning of life.

B. J. and I parted in '55, when my family packed off to a missionary venture in South America. Since that day I have lived in thirty-three homes, some more memorable than others. B. J. has lived in his home town all his life and is, I think, in his second home. B. J.'s roots go deep in his town.

The passing of a generation, the birth and growth of another—all of this transpires with a certain order when you are stationary the way someone like B. J. is. For most of us, though, it is a case of "turn around and you're young; turn around and you're grown." We keep moving, if not spinning, and the passage of generations takes place in the process.

I envy B. J. on my moving days. There is something about gathering up your stuff *again*—two moves is the same as one fire, they say—that brings a tear to the eye. This moving business is a hint of our mortality. Certainly it is a reminder of how paltry the stuff in our closets is. The temptation to abandon it all to the next tenant is almost irresistible. I tell myself, at least put a "garage sale" sign out front. Take it all. Leave me some books and a favorite chair. The rest you can have if you'll just take it.

Still, we movers have our roots. There are the few choice places you go back to and savor the feelings again. Memory is kind enough to erase much of the pain of life, and we remember mostly the joy. The scent of autumn leaves can transport me back to the carefree days of autumn in old Ottawa with B. J. playing on into the frosty evenings around an old museum with friends, hurling the frisbee-like projectiles we had made out of popsicle sticks into the darkening sky, watching for the swallows to dart out of their elevated houses and fend them off. I love just walking around visiting my old sites when a conference takes me back. Almost all of my many home towns beckon me back. Just living in the pleasant memories of these familiar settings is a very sheltering thing to me.

While the physical roots are pleasant, not enough of my old

neighborhoods are preserved intact. But that's not all that's changed. The family farm on Ruth's side is having an implement auction this very week. The land that Jim Lucas, Ruth's great-grandfather, bought and broke back in 1880 now has no heir to work it. Jim's son turned the land into a first-class dairy farm with 100 head of choice Jerseys. Then, when he turned it over to his son, Arnold, it became an ultra-modern production center, the pride of the county.

Uncle Arn died this year. Everything had to be sold, and over 1000 people attended the auction. There is an enormous sadness over the demise of a family farm. I suppose it's the roots.

We need a sense of roots that is greater than houses, land, and towns, a heritage that shelters life in a way that is deeper than the earth. It has a little to do with genes, maybe, and a lot to do with the values that have come down to us. And it comes from our spiritual heritage. In a sense, I live in the shadows of my father and grandparents, even though they have passed off the scene. I am reminded of this in the covenant that God made to Abraham: "Because you have done this thing, and have not withheld your son, your only son, in blessing I will bless you, and in multiplying I will multiply your descendants as the stars of the heaven and as the sand which is on the seashore; and your descendants shall possess the gate of their enemies. In your seed all the nations of the earth shall be blessed, because you have obeyed My voice" (Gen. 22:16–18). Abraham's descendants would reap the benefits of his obedience. They would be successful in battle. They would enjoy prosperity. It would be the carry-over of God's blessings on Abraham.

My father, E. Howard, was an Abraham figure to me. He made hard choices related to mission work that many of us would have avoided. And I am the beneficiary of his obedience.

> When in the night He calls my name
> And I must answer "Lord, send me."
> Great seems the cost, and small the gain,
> So foolish seems the step to be.

Hardship ahead, a rugged way,
No life of comfort promised me;
But list the challenge ringing clear:
"Even Thy Lord faced Calvary."

Long doth the battle fiercely rage,
Heart-ties beckon and self persuade,
Then, like a calm at even-tide,
His will accepted—choice is made.

Down at His feet surrendered lie
Talents and powers—a life out-poured,
And 'spite and suff'ring, pain and loss,
I'll take the hard way, Master Lord![2]

Another of my father's poems reminds me of this commitment to
the hard way which is my heritage:

"Chosen of Christ"—O princely commission,
May its high purpose in me ne'er grow dim.
Training or marching, suff'ring or dying,
Always a soldier—may I please Him![3]

We are the beneficiary of E. Howard's obedience, my sisters and I,
in many ways: The knowledge of Latin culture and language is
ingrained deeply enough that all of us like to live in Spanish countries. I think we are comfortable in almost any culture. We have
experienced another culture on a depth that far exceeds anything a
stationary education experience could produce. And then there are
E. Howard's values. When we get too comfortable with middle-
class Christianity, North American style, we tend to hear calls in
the night.

I watched Jeff, our 17-year-old son, standing in an airport
lineup with his fellow band-members. They were off to Disney-
land. You are one lucky kid, I thought. You are the beneficiary of
your grandfather's obedience. This lad also, I think, will over-
come. His life will bless nations. I have no doubt of that. The
rewards of obedience follow well down the line.

This sense of rootedness in a great man's character lends a kind of protection to all of life. "What would Dad do?" I often ask myself. Even without that conscious asking, E. Howard's Christian character often governs mine. I know instinctively that envy or smallness would find no place in his great spirit. His aversion to materialism, while living with a grand, expansive spirit, is something I aspire to. His marvelous skills in diplomacy, which ingratiated him to people around the world, come to mind when I am tempted to let somebody have it, to dash off multi-copied letters and start a small riot. Dad settled disputes in person, with plenty of smiles covering his firmness. "You have to do the right thing" he would say. "A man has to live with himself." Integrity, love, propriety, willingness to dare—these are qualities I have seen modeled up close. My roots are sunk deep into his character.

With that allegiance to a person, there is a certain allegiance to his beliefs and people. The fact that it was good enough for him, makes it good enough for me. I certainly sense great weight attached to some of his preferences. Such is E. Howard's influence over me to this day that even in middle-age I find it painful to disappoint him. So, I am connected, not just to a person who continues to cast a giant shadow over my life from beyond this life, but I am connected to a denomination because it was his, to a lifestyle, a church body, a fellowship, a circle of connecting people—all because these too are part of the heritage. The pace of change going on around me may continue to bother me, but it doesn't threaten me because I have those roots. I also have a foundation that reaches further back than even my father and grandparents. You have it, too.

"Look to the rock from which you were hewn," said Isaiah, "and to the hole of the pit from which you were dug."

> *Look to Abraham your father,*
> *And to Sarah who bore you;*
> *For I called him alone,*
> *And blessed him and increased him."*
> (Isa. 51:1–2)

That is your heritage, the prophet said to his people, Judah. A solitary, transient man, willing to be fully obedient, Abraham became the "father of many nations." And the blessings of Abraham spill over to his descendants.

> *For the Lord will comfort Zion,*
> *He will comfort all her waste places;*
> *He will make her wilderness like Eden*
> *And her desert like the garden of the LORD;*
> *Joy and gladness will be found in it,*
> *Thanksgiving and the voice of melody."* (Isa. 51:3)

The assurance of restoration and blessing in the present stems from the obedience of one great ancestor in the past.

Of course, the New Testament truth is that all people of faith are the descendants of Abraham and heirs to the blessings that follow him: "Therefore know that only those who are of faith are sons of Abraham. And the Scripture, foreseeing that God would justify the nations by faith, preached the gospel to Abraham beforehand, saying *'In you all nations shall be blessed'*. So then those who are of faith are blessed with believing Abraham" (Gal. 3:7–9). These are great roots that are available to the most rootless of us in our transient world. When all else crumbles, when nothing seems familiar or permanent anymore, we have a stronghold of character and virtue that comes down to us from a great past. We are part of the most noble lineage possible as we are linked by faith with the father of the faithful.

Similarly, Paul reminded the Ephesians that, "you are no longer strangers and foreigners, but fellow citizens with the saints and members of the household of God, having been built on the foundation of the apostles and prophets, Jesus Christ himself being the chief cornerstone" (Eph. 2:19–20). A living faith connects one with the most permanent roots.

For Isaiah, as for us, this was a most appealing image. Despite the decimation of the times, the fragmentation which had left his people broken and lost, there were marvelous possibilities for regathering and rebuilding:

Those from among you
Shall build the old waste places;
You shall raise up the foundations of many generations;
And you shall be called the Repairer of the Breach,
The Restorer of Streets to Dwell In. . . .
And I will cause you to ride on the high hills of the
*   earth,*
And feed you with the heritage of Jacob your father.
The mouth of the LORD has spoken." (Isa. 58:12–14)

We need to receive such prophetic assurances ourselves these days. There are immeasurable rewards for people of obedience and faith, not the least of which is a sense of roots. Our lives can be lived with a sense of connection to the great men and women of our past. We connect with them as we connect with our common Lord.

People who are touched by the Messiah are like "trees of righteousness, the planting of the Lord":

And they shall rebuild the old ruins,
They shall raise up the former desolations,
And they shall repair the ruined cities,
The desolations of many generations. (Isa. 61:3–4)

Part 7

Shelter Is Having a Shepherd

Sometimes I miss school days. There was something about having a teacher I really wanted to please that made the time memorable and I remember it now with pleasure. Of course, occasionally when there was a teacher I cared little about pleasing, or, for that matter, ever seeing again, my attitude changed somewhat. But there were special people along the way, such as Miss Woods in grade four and Mr. Vibart in grade ten, that I admired so much there was no limit to what I would do to impress.

Who do we try to please these days? What kinds of shepherds enter our adult lives in a similar way? I find I miss that old desire to please, to go the second mile to make an impression on someone I admire. I have overseers of sorts, but it's just not the same. Mostly, I oversee myself, but sometimes I would like to be more account-able to someone. I would like that person to say, "Have you done your homework? Are you learning what you should be learning?" Why is no one asking me those questions anymore?

What we miss with the passing of teacher-overseers is another form of security. We knew when we were school children that if we did an assignment well, were attentive to instructions, and followed directions, we would produce work that was acceptable and affirming.

In adult life too much of what we do goes unnoticed. We lose that gratifying, secure sense of growing under someone's watchful eye. Some of us, more than others, long for a teacher, but we all need a shepherd.

Chapter 21

An Overseer, a King

Many people have bosses, and some are their own boss. Given the choice, quite a few prefer to have bosses. There are times, in fact, that as a pastor I wouldn't mind being an employee. I'd like to leave all the strategic stuff, the long-term planning, the day-to-day supervision in the hands of a superior who would simply tell me what to do. Sometimes it sounds very appealing.

Then I remember how Erich Fromm, in his classic book *Escape from Freedom,* described the daunting challenges of being your own boss:

> What are the social and economic factors in society that make for the striving for freedom? Can freedom become a burden, too heavy for man to bear, something he tries to escape from? Why then is it that freedom is for many a cherished goal and for others a threat?
>
> Is there not also, perhaps, besides an innate desire for freedom, an instinctive wish for submission? If there is not, how can we account for the attraction which submission to a leader has for so many today? Is submission always to an overt authority, or is there also submission to internalized authorities, such as duty or conscience, to inner compulsions or to anonymous authorities like public opinion? Is there a hidden satisfaction in submitting, and what is its essence?[1]

There is something in our human nature that longs to submit to authority. Maybe that is why we find it so reassuring to have a benign overseer. Not the supervisor at one office I know, who drives half the employees crazy with his conflicting instructions and meddlesomeness, but the kind who really has the large interests of the company and the good of the employees at heart. Always making decisions without a superior, when there are no checks and no parameters, can be very dissipating. We need authority figures we can bounce off of. Even if the person we answer to is too overbearing, the resentment generated can produce good things—a great thrust for new ventures, perhaps even a new company. Many a great revolution has been sparked by rebellion against arrogant authority figures.

One of the colleges of my past was an authoritarian place, complete with a "six-inch-rule," which pertained either to hemlines or to the distance between the sexes according to the occasion and the application. Once I was ready to lead a revolt. There were punctuality rules, including a curfew. There were rules regarding hair length and dress. There were rules governing leisure time.

Goodness, the resentment that place generated! Some of us spent a good part of the year in protest—written protest, spoken protest, private and public, verbal and active. The year deteriorated into a series of non-violent actions. Often there were sheer defiance of the laws and laughing compliance with the resulting punishment.

Now, much later and from a different vantage, I see the good of that repressive environment. It squeezed our values. It made us howl in protest, issuing the call for freedom. Let *us* make those decisions, we cried. Don't ask us to obey rules on which we have not been consulted. It forced into the open our ingrained resentment of senseless legalism. And having found such strong early expression, anti-legalism is still very important to me, like a great unwritten rule.

On the other hand, I found the strict codes of a British high school, complete with the decree to wear navy blazers, grey flannels, and ties, utterly just and right. I was young then, and we didn't hear howls of protest from adolescents in the fifties. But I also had a sense of having found my place in a vast social order. I was on the bottom rung, of course, at least in my early years there. Prefects and Sub-Prefects, the boys from the higher grades, lorded over us quite mercilessly. We were their errand-boys on demand. They were entitled to bash the younger boys around quite freely in the name of keeping order during the lunch hours or in the class-rooms before lectures began.

Above the prefect level were the teachers, the lords of the manor. They would administer The Cane, as I found out. And they could humiliate a student to the point of tears over some minor offense or other. I suspect they were not highly qualified, but I came out of the place with a great love for Shakespearean drama and rugby—and for the great teeming life of a boys' school.

Most feared of all was the legendary D. V., the Headmaster of St. Alban's College. Pity the boy who crossed D. V. He was said to apply the cane ferociously, or even to attack with shoes and books. And when he glowered upon you with those fierce eyes burning under bushy brows, old D. V. instilled the very fear of the Almighty.

"Take your hands out of your pockets when I'm talking to you!" he bellowed at me one sunny afternoon, like a bull heard across several farm yards. I was drifting back from a leisurely visit to the washroom. I straightened up in a hurry and marched smartly back to class, venturing a sidelong glance at him only when I reached the door of the classroom. Those fierce eyes were still glowering menacingly at me, following me right inside the door. I was so shaken up, stricken so dumb, I could barely lift my pencil for the rest of the day. I would not so much as acknowledge my friend's whisper and that made him and his colleagues laugh heartily at my brush with death. I still quake inside at the thought of D. V.

Nobody instills that kind of fear these days, do they? At my son's recent graduation from high school, the head table was occupied by bland company men who would hardly instill fear in a fourth grader. There was no fierceness there. Their words were carefully chosen and smooth. There were no threats, no bombast. How do you run a school without making kids feel the force of authority? Unless there is parental authority in a school system pushing kids from behind, so to speak, the students can disappear. Attend a class or do not; be involved in athletics or not; take that program or not. Everything is optional. Supposedly young people are learning the consequences of their own decisions. I would rather have them learning the fear of God.

Debbie chose to quit. It was only four months before graduation, but she had missed so many classes, the prospect of graduating had disappeared. Where was everyone when she was missing all those classes? Attending to other things? Caught up in their own problems? There was no one who cared enough to make sure good things were happening for Debbie that year.

Without the weight of authority upon us, we forget we are cared for. I knew I mattered when someone insisted that I be in class. I knew many decisions were made for me. At that tender age that was exactly what I needed. All I had to decide was to get my homework done and show up. It was simple, and it was safe.

We may need more regimentation in our lives than we have. Perhaps the Toffler assessment of our fragmented times points us in the direction of authority. We need to bring ourselves under discipline without sacrificing our freedom. We need somehow to manage the infinite choices before us.

My challenge is to be ruled more religiously by my datebook. If something is not done on the assigned day, I need to give it top billing on the following, and so on. I allow the thing to order me around a bit.

When you are your own boss, it is rewarding to enroll in regular prescribed things for the sake of your sense of obligation. Taking a university course, for example, pulls me into a regimented, evenly paced world where there is a beginning and an end, with several assignments in-between.

Some of my colleagues like to make themselves accountable to one another. It increases their sense of having an overseer and it is a spiritual exercise. One gentleman is always inviting people to "speak into" his life. He believes direction comes best from without.

Within the walls of my British high school, we enjoyed an infinitely interesting life. All the ingredients of a reasonable education were there, complete with the tumultuous matters of hostility and relationships. Sitting in the Argentine sun, a cluster of boys awaiting the bell that summoned us to class, we were a contented lot. By today's standards, we were utterly regimented. We lined up for inspection every morning; we sang the national anthem. But in that regimentation was shelter.

"Behold a king will reign righteously," said Isaiah, "and princes will rule justly. And each will be like a refuge from the wind, and a shelter from the storm" (Isa. 32:1–2). That is authority at its best. To be ruled by a messianic king, one for whom justice is top priority, is to enjoy wonderful shelter: "My people will live in a peaceful habitation, in secure dwellings and in quiet resting places" (Isa. 32:18).

God is committed to establishing such rule. It is "the zeal of the Lord of hosts" that establishes and upholds the throne. When that zeal is removed, we "stray from the ways, and harden our heart from fearing thee. "We have become like those of old over whom you never ruled, those who were not called by your name" (Isa. 63:19). In our democratic times, we must acknowledge our need to bow down. Without the weight of authority upon us, we cannot experience shelter at its best.

Chapter 22

The Shepherd

Every so often I get reminded that as a pastor I am a shepherd. And it is sobering. Recently at our pastoral seminar, a guest speaker startled all of us with "Woe to the worthless shepherds!" If he wanted to startle us, to wake us up, to get our attention, he was quite successful. It was a long seminar.

The point was that we have the responsibility to tend God's people and, like the Master Shepherd, we must be constant in our responsibilities. God speaks to us through Jeremiah and says, "Woe to the shepherds who destroy and scatter the sheep of My pasture! You have scattered my flock, driven them away, and not attended to them" (Jer. 23:1–2).

You might ask, how could that happen? Don't shepherds always tend their flocks carefully, searching endlessly for the one sheep that is lost? Jeremiah has the answer: "The shepherds have become dull-hearted and have not sought the LORD; therefore they shall not prosper, and all their flocks shall be scattered" (Jer. 10:21). It is a true jeremiad.

Yet, it is good to remind us of our roles. There is the call to attend to the flock, to be mindful of their needs. There is the pursuit, the gathering, the pastoral care. What a calling this is.

Shepherding seems almost extinct. It is threatened by the self-interest that, as we were reminded at our seminar, invades even the clergy. It is threatened by a variety of duties that push basic shepherding to the back burner. It is threatened by the increasing professionalism of the times, which has young ministers focused more on methodology than pastoral care. It has fallen victim to the church-growth movement, with its stress on multi-staffing and flocks beyond number, never mind naming. Shepherding has fallen on hard times. Often enough for me it succumbs to the needs of privacy.

Still, that's what we pastors are—shepherds. We may act more like bankers, but the essential vocation is to shepherd. Unless we are taking care of people, we are not doing our jobs. Pastors are called to "take heed to yourselves and to all the flock . . . to shepherd the church of God" (Acts 20:28). We are to seek the "little ones" (see Matt. 18:10) who may have gotten lost, as the shepherd in the parable seeks the one lost sheep. Doing that kind of work, shepherds serve as "examples to the flock" (see 1 Pet. 5:3).

My motivation for spending pastoral time with people gets a boost now and then in various ways. One was a card Linda sent to me after I'd spent pastoral time with her.

> Dear Pastor,
> Just a note to let you know that you are appreciated and respected very much. Your influence in my life has been a blessing!
>
> > God bless,
> > Linda

Linda's note reminds me that *I am a shepherd,* regardless of how strung out I may be on a given day. It is my presence that affects her, not the amount of time I spend with her. I think I detect appreciation for the consistency of my lifestyle when she is having the most unpredictable of times. Some kind of consistency, friendly admonition, a gentle spirit—people look to pastors for such things.

So, I resolve to spend more time with people and not delegate that to a staff person. I like to take a day and spend it on the streets like a salesman—no staff meetings, no family meetings outside of a shared meal. This is my "people day." And even though some visits are too short, some on the run, some rather routine and dull, there is always a reward when arriving on someone's door. David said that he who rules in righteousness is like the dawn. I am not a ruler; I am a shepherd. But I sometimes see the light of dawn in the faces of people. They like to see their shepherd.

"You're like an angel from heaven today," said old Mary McKenzie from her rocker. I thought she was laying it on a little thick, but I smiled and felt good anyway. It turned out she wanted to use a heating pad for a lingering chest cold and couldn't reach the electrical outlet! Such a small thing for the shepherd; such an important need for Mary.

My flagging pastoral zeal is restored also by remembering. Thoughts of my own shepherds are an encouragement to be faithful myself. There was my father, who modeled a godly life in my growing up years as well as later. When my father would lead a worship service and bring his expository mind to bear on a text, I felt all was well with the world. That process brought order to my life more times than I can count. There was refuge just in his being there enunciating the changeless themes of the scripture. It was one of those enclaves where the pace of change and corruption is arrested.

Dad had a way of looking at people that told them they mattered. He had a twinkle in his eyes that drew people to him. I think his genuine interest in all people was what evoked such admiration from his growing flocks.

Looking back now, I realize I have not had enough pastors. I began my life with a father/pastor. Now I have a self/pastor. And there was very little pastoring done in between. Oh, there were college chaplains and a fleeting figure or two during brief stops along the way, but none that touched my life. I probably needed more pastoring. Come to think of it, from time to time I need pastoring right now.

I have an overseer who serves as pastor to the pastors of my area. He is one good man. I look on him as a friend. But, he too has to delegate the shepherding role sometimes. Recently his administrative assistant has been appointed Director of Pastoral Care, so that the superintendent can give more of his time to enhancing church growth. The appointment seems to be in keeping with the assistant's gifts and all, but it also perpetuates the blight. This may be one thing we just cannot delegate. I believe that is certainty true in the local church.

The idea of God as shepherd is an appealing one throughout the Old Testament. He goes before his flock (see Ps. 68:7) and guides it (see Ps. 23:3); he leads it to pasture (see Jer. 50:19) and places it where it can rest by the waters (see Ps. 23:2 and 80:1); he protects it with his staff (see Ps. 23:4); he whistles to the dispersed (see Zech. 10:8) and gathers them (see Isa. 56:8). It is one of the most sheltering images of God that we have.

Most often this image of God as shepherd is found in the consoling prophecies of the Exile. In Jeremiah God says, "I myself will gather the remnant of My flock out of all the countries where I have driven them, and bring them back to their folds; and they shall be fruitful and increase" (Jer. 23:3). And in Ezekiel he says, "I Myself will search for My sheep and seek them out. As a shepherd cares for his herd in the day when he is among his scattered sheep, so will I care for my sheep and I will deliver them from all the places to which they were scattered on a cloudy and gloomy day. And I will bring them out from the peoples" (Ezek. 34:11–13).

Isaiah brought his image of God as shepherd onto the scene in a great statement of comfort, when he revealed God's words to him:

> *Comfort, O comfort my people,*
> *   says your God.*
> *Speak kindly to Jerusalem;*
> *And call out to her, that her warfare*
> *   has ended.* (Isa. 40:1–2)

Outside of Psalm 23, there is no more hopeful dwelling on this concept of the Almighty. Judah had been trampled and scattered. All hope of a strong homeland was lost. From there, of all places, comes the great consolation: God is our shepherd and cares for us with painstaking diligence and love:

> *Thus says the Lord, "In a favored time*
> *I have answered You,*

*And in a day of salvation I have
    helped you;
And I will . . . restore the land, to make
    them inherit the desolate heritages; . . .
Along the roads they will feed,
And their pasture will be on all
    bare heights. . . . .
For He who has compassion on them
    will lead them,
And will guide them to springs of water"*
    (Isa. 49:8–10)

The shepherd ministry of the church is especially for the ravaged. Just as it is seen most often in the consoling prophecy of the Exile, this image needs to be felt by the dispersed and broken of our own time. It is the victim of desertion that needs to know that God is a shepherd. The sick, the abandoned, the one ravaged by drugs, the one who has spent so long in the wilderness he has lost all memory of the fold, the lonely aged, long driven away from their roots and friends, the abandoned, those whose sense of self-worth has been lost in the cheap exchanges of life's bartering table, the alcoholic, the prostitute—it is to all such that this reality of God as shepherd must come to bear. Too often, "the reality" is a very well-protected, well-groomed flock and shepherd who are quite oblivious to the dispersed. We enjoy the sheltering awareness of God without expressing his seeking, restoring nature.

No one should ever feel pushed out beyond the sphere of the church's shelter. As a shepherd present in the world, the church is especially *for* the downtrodden, the despairing, the weak and the broken. During our times of brokenness, we must draw upon the strength that the church affords. Sometimes this means pushing through the lineup of well-fed flock members at the trough. But we help recall the church to its essential mission when rather than give up on it, we call it to attend to the scattered.

We church members should heed the call to be shepherds. God will never be known as the great shepherd of human lives unless we represent him that way. We are his hands, his feet, his arms, scepter, and fold. Opening up our facilities to the unchurched is a must, trying though it may be. There are means that make us "seeker friendly" that we must continue to exploit. The more pains we take to make this statement, "this church is a great fold for the trampled, downtrodden, scattered, and oppressed," the closer we will be to fulfilling our mission.

Part 8

Shelter as Covering

Patches of shade—from Buenos Aires to Barcelona, with a lot of Canadian countryside in between—these little pockets of peace have afforded memorable moments on hot days. One of the disappointments with travel is always the "occupied" sign. You find the thing on washrooms at the worst moments. But imagine our disappointment, on a blazing Barcelona day, to find the shade occupied. We had been strolling the beach area for some time when I began to feel something like heat prostration setting in. There were few enough large trees as it was. But virtually every tree was host to five families sprawled on lawnchairs and blankets. A patch of shade was a scarce commodity. I hadn't expected to find the shade "occupied."

Like many biblical writers, the psalmist finds dense shelter in the sense of being overshadowed: "He who dwells in the shelter of the Most High will abide in the shadow of the Almighty" (Ps. 91:1). The Lord provides a covering from the heat. And we, in turn, are called to provide that for others. It is the same as Christ's teaching, "I am the light of the world," and then, "You are the light." Having experienced his marvelous light, we are enabled to provide light for others. So it is with shade. We experience God's overshadowing presence in order to become shade for the exposed lives around us.

But none of this would be possible were it not for the covering we find in God's Son. Isaiah portrays the Suffering Servant as the most exposed figure imaginable. And yet it is his exposure to the full brunt of the wrath of God that provides the most complete shelter that man can ever know. The climax of Isaiah's shelter theme is the exposure of the Suffering Servant and the "covering" that he provides.

Chapter 23

Shade by Day

One of the most cherished moments of shelter I have had was in Jericho. (Fortunately I was not inside the walls, which proved to be rather inadequate shelter, as we recall.) As we walked through the ruins, the sun had been beating down as only that Jordan valley sun can. The temperature was something like forty degrees centigrade, and I was ducking into every patch of shade I could find. Then we found the delightful coolness of a simple shelter: bamboo lengths laid across some poles tied across a span between four posts. How could heaven be so elementary? Who would have thought that rows of thin, split bamboo cane could produce such cool and delightful refuge? Sitting in that shade, we sipped some cool water and gazed out at the scorched rocky soil all around us, the parched desert across the Jordan where Joshua had assembled his invaders, the dried up ghost town nearby. The desert wind, which seemed to suck the life out of us outside, was just a pleasant breeze inside.

I find a sense of being overshadowed is my most profound experience of God. While the exuberant times are most stimulating, like the timbrel and harp the psalmist speaks of or the wave of corporate praise that sweeps over a congregation, they do not contribute as strong a sense of God's presence to me as the descending pressure I identify with being overshadowed.

One such time was when a man named Arbizu visited our Argentine mission compound. I must have been all of fifteen. At the close of that service it was as though the weight of God's hand was laid upon me. Not a sound came from my lips. I did not make a gesture of praise. It was a crushing, silencing presence. To speak a syllable would have seemed irreverent. I was overshadowed by the weighty presence of God.

These days, we tend to treat God with a kind of backslapping camaraderie. The very idea of the awesome presence of God is recognized mainly in his absence. I see good things happening in shared prayer times and expressive worship, yet I remain a spokesman for an experience of his overshadowing that is silencing and overpowering. "Thou has beset me behind and before and laid thy hand upon me," says the psalmist. Once he lays hold of your life that way, there is no escape.

Occasionally, I have this sense. It is always when I am alone. It may be when I am in prayer, or even when I am crossing a pedestrian bridge on a sunny afternoon. I am arrested again. I know there is no escape. That hand presses down, and I am dazzled with the divine again.

The hero of Camus's *The Outsider* is always grated by the sun. It oppresses and agitates him. Perhaps it is a symbol of the God he has rejected or the harsh, overbearing realities of life. For Camus they are crushing. "Mother died today. Or maybe yesterday; I can't be sure." These opening lines establish a troubled and disordered mind trying to cope with the harsh realities. But always the sun oppresses him. "It was a blazing hot afternoon . . . the glare off the road and from the sky, the reek of petrol and the jolts." At the vigil, "the glare from the white walls was making my eyes smart." At the funeral, "The sky was already a blaze of light, and the air stoking up rapidly. I felt the first waves of heat lapping my back, and my dark suit made things worse. . . . Now, in the full glare of the morning sun, with everything shimmering in the heat haze, there was something inhuman, discouraging about this landscape."[1]

God provides a shelter from the stark, oppressive heat of the day. A blazing sun is like the harsh realities of the twentieth century: economic collapse, massive starvation, global warming, economic disparity, environmental trouble, overpopulation, nuclear holocaust, racism, the glaring light of secular humanism. These glaring facts blaze out at modern man like Camus's sun. We need a buffer zone, a shaded area, through which to absorb these harsh realities. How can these be assimilated without some kind of filtered light?

God's presence is an environment for faith. He filters the glaring hurts of life through himself and thus offers a context for belief. It is only under the shelter of strong faith that we can properly assess the realities of times like our own. Exposed to the blazing evidence of man's inhumanity to man and his world, we are as inclined to hopelessness as Camus's young hero on the loss of his mother. But filtered through the foliage of faith, there is a softer light in which we can continue to believe in a loving purpose for life.

When Isaiah looked around at the political landscape of his day, his vision was bleak. His little nation was subjected to enormous oppression. The surrounding nations were a continual threat. He knew that apart from divine intervention, ultimately Judah must fall.

But God provides shelter. When the enemies turned up the heat of their oppression, Judah experienced special shade and Isaiah praised God:

> *For You have been a strength to the poor,*
> *A strength for the needy in his distress,*
> *A refuge from the storm,*
> *A shade from the heat;*
> *For the blast of the terrible ones is as a storm*
>   *against the wall.*
> *You will reduce the noise of aliens,*
> *As heat in a dry place;*
> *As heat in the shadow of a cloud,*
> *The song of the terrible will be diminished.*
>   (Isa. 25:4–5)

There is another great force from which there is no protection.

Worse than the hot breath of the ruthless oppressor is the blazing sun of divine judgment itself. When your shade has become the oppressing sun, where do you turn? This is the prospect that faced rebellious Judah. She would be purged. Ultimately her shade would be removed.

But then came a new day. There are flashes of this restored kingdom in Isaiah, a re-established, peaceful nation back in its homeland after the Exile. And this rebuilt nation would again experience rich shelter: "And there will be a tabernacle for shade in the daytime from the heat for a place of refuge, and for a shelter from storm and rain" (Isa. 4:6). The purging of Zion is now passed and the holy remnant of Israel will enjoy the "fruit of the earth." Their blessedness is guaranteed by an overshadowing presence of God, not unlike the fire and cloudy pillar which led their ancestors out of Egypt: "The Lord will create above every dwelling place of Mount Zion . . . a cloud and smoke by day and the shining of flaming fire by night. For over all the glory will be a covering (Isa. 4:5). To Isaiah such overshadowing is synonymous with blessedness.

We can certainly identify with the heat Isaiah feels. Sometimes the blast of the ruthless hits very close to home and we feel what it is like to be hemmed against a wall by a desert storm. We have one ruthless adversary, to be sure, who likes nothing better than to turn up the heat on us. Hemmed in, desperate to escape, feeling the very life sucked out of us—times of test can be very much like being caught in a drought or a desert storm.

"I come in second so many times," says Bill, my one-time executive friend. "Unfortunately, second is the same as last in this business. You either get the contract or you don't." He's in the "executive placement" business. And a year of second place finishes leaves even a robust faith like Bill's badly bruised. He is in a pressure cooker right now, in mid-life, where even attending a career-planning seminar seems like a luxury he can ill-afford.

"You need some space," I found myself saying to him recently, "where you can think about your future. If this is career change, as it seems to be, you need some freedom from financial hassles to be able to make the right decisions." Instead of "space," I might have called it "shade." How do you make the best decisions without it? That is like trying to find your directions when you are caught between the pavement and the blazing sun.

We need an environment of coolness, a place of reflection, when the heat of life is turned up. Shade offers a respite from intense heat where you can slow the pace and breathe deeply.

On the practical level, this shade may be the quietness of a devotional life. The interlacing of scripture and prayer provides a sheltered place where we can reflect. We can ponder the options open to us in a context of comfort and renewal. We can leave our sheltered spot with fresh energies to take to the road.

This shade also suggests a filter. Light still gets through a leafy arbor, but it is filtered light. Unfiltered the glaring realities of twentieth century life are too intense for us. It is like staring into the blazing face of the sun itself without eye protection. But faith provides the necessary filter. We can look at the facts of age and mortality, as Abraham did, and "waver not through unbelief." We see the realities of life through the filter of faith.

Shade is also transforming. A horrible day can be transformed into a splendid one by the imposition of shade. The scorching wind, "the breath of the ruthless," as Isaiah puts it, becomes a gentle, refreshing breeze under the shadows of this shelter. The amazing capacity of God to transform things is never more apparent than here. The psalmist says, "You have turned my mourning into dancing." It is not just a matter of easing the pain, but of replacing the pain with ecstasy.

Mostly a pocket of shade is renewing. After a long enough flop in a leafy shelter, I was ready to mount my ten-speed again and continue a week-long bike hike through the hills of Ontario. Our Lord calls us to himself to experience this restoring power. It is in his orbit that our strength is renewed.

The loss of shade is the great challenge of our day. The desertification of Africa has much to do with the chopping up of scant vegetation for fuel. This destruction of the rain forests portends consequences that we cannot fully grasp. The world is being increasingly exposed. I visit my neighboring province of British Columbia and see great patches of clear-basing in the forests where trees have been harvested all over the hillsides, leaving bare, rocky blotches amid the greenery. We feel this loss when we return to our cities after a walk in the woods chirping with life.

I feel the loss of shade.

When I am drawn by the deep shadows, I recall the words of Emerson:

> Think me not unkind and rude
> That I walk alone in grove and glen;
> I go to the God of the wood
> To fetch his word to men.[2]

Chapter 24

Shelter for Others

My favorite ice cream store provides more than fifty flavors, and its mango and Irish cream "split single" is an item that pops into my fantasies on almost any hot day. It is a truly "cool" place. There is the air-conditioned comfort, of course. And there is the old oak pew you can flop down on while you lick away for a time. There is the old player piano in the corner. Spend ten minutes in that cool interior and you are ready to face the hottest summer afternoon again.

There are also people who provide us with the qualities of cool shade. They stand over our lives like great oak trees, looking down from their places in history or space on our experience, casting a refreshing influence over all we do. A great moral stance gives them this quality. People like Martin Luther King are a respite to us in our growing cynicism. There *are* virtues worth living for, surely, if some have been willing to die for them.

A cheerful and buoyant disposition has this same quality of shade about it. The office of a travel agent I know is a most pleasant environment. This man, with his naturally flushed complexion, exudes such *joie de vivre* with his sparkling twinkle, infectious smile, and uproarious laugh. You come from his office feeling that all is well with the world after all.

I was blessed with a father who provided that kind of shade for as long as I can remember. It has to do with his commitment to me as a person. You sit down with someone like him for an evening and talk family, friends, shop. You feel again the warmth of life-long affection. Gradually, you want to work your way around to the knotty issues that brought you there. "Here are my options, Dad. A decision has to be made. What do you advise?" But by the time you get to it, often the problem has been incredibly reduced. The process of small talk has shrunk it and it is not nearly as grating as it was. The urgency is gone. In this refreshing cool context of love, you can handle almost anything.

We tend to talk *around* our issues as much as speak *to* them. But this indirect approach has much to commend it. It creates an environment where a right decision can be made: an environment of faith and love, of confidence in a support network—a cool climate where you talk while you peel apples or split peas. It is the breadth of Dad's experience, I think, of his full tasting of life, that gave his life the quality of shade.

Coolness is the dominant quality of shade. A "cool guy" does not rush into things frenetically. He assesses the demands of life in the context of his own pace and priorities. You can invade his space with the most pressing demands, but his coolness will likely prevail. The urgent issue will be refrigerated. It will come under the power of the important.

This is a beautiful, high calling. To provide a cool environment for people, a place to reflect, to filter out the demands of life, to see the pressing issues cool down, the grating blast transformed into refreshing breezes—what could be a more worthy enterprise?

Isaiah sets before us this kind of role. Picturing the messianic kingdom, he says,

> *A man will be as a hiding place from the wind,*
> *And a cover from the tempest,*
> *As rivers of water in a dry place,*
> *As the shadow of a great rock in a weary land.* (32:2)

And in the meantime, there is urgent work to be done. It is not enough to serve God in ritual, trampling the temple courts with an endless stream of sacrifices or calling for fasts. Fasting, says

Isaiah, means more than bowing one's head "like a reed" and "spreading out sackcloth and ashes as a bed."

> *Is not this the fast which I chose,*
> *To loosen the bonds of wickedness,*
> *To undo the bands of the yoke,*
> *And to let the oppressed go free,*
> *And break every yoke?*
> *Is it not to divide your bread with the hungry,*
> *And bring the homeless poor into the house;*
> *When you see the naked to cover him*
> *And not to hide yourself from your own*
> *flesh?* (Isa. 58:5–7 NASV)

This is the prophetic call for justice described in terms of shelter. To clothe the naked and bring the homeless poor under your roof— this, says Isaiah, is true worship of God.

Of course, a very similar theme is sounded in Jesus' parable of the sheep and the goats. "I was a stranger and you invited me in," says the King to the righteous. "I needed clothes and you clothed me." When? ask the righteous. The King replies, "Whatever you did for one of these brothers of mine, even the least of them, you did it to me" (see Matt. 25:35–40).

The exposure of great masses of people in our world today presses in daily on our consciousness. The sight of people starving under a blazing African sun is painful and troubling to all of us. They stand as symbols of the millions whose lives are baked out of them by the heat of the circumstances of poverty, abuse, homelessness, systematic oppression, misfortune, family breakdown, and desertion. The shade they need strengthens the call of scripture to us. To provide shade is to go beyond handouts. It is to *stand between* a person and the forces that threaten to destroy him. It means absorbing the heat of the problem yourself, so that she may have respite.

This is substitution, and it is a long way from our rather detached responses to the ravaged poor of our time. We dole out things—food, cast-off belongings, medicines, money, advice, a night at the hostel—but do we stand between the oppressed and the forces against them? That we can do only with direct involvement. Personal contact is the only way we can provide this kind of shelter. You have to feel the heat in order to provide shade for someone else.

We kid ourselves when we substitute all kinds of worship forms for direct involvement with the poor. Through Isaiah God asks, Who needs your fasts? Much too often we settle for the long reach and the cool touch, but there *is no substitute* for direct involvement with the oppressed.

A short stay in hospital can help you appreciate gospel television. Lying there among the sick, afflicted yourself, is when you can soak it up properly. You have the time to think about a program and to respond. You can assess the impact of today's most pervasive form of evangelism. You can see how intimately it touches.

During my recent ten days in the hospital, recovering from a bit of minor surgery, I exposed myself to the full impact of Sunday morning gospel TV, possibly for the first and last times. I tried to put myself in the place of my roommates. Could it reach them?

Programming led off with the morning service of "The People's Church." It was Thanksgiving Sunday and we viewers shared the spirit of the choir's "Jesus, We Just Want to Thank You." Pastor Paul Smith's message, "Thanks Be To God for His Unspeakable Gift!" was clear and simple. He pointed various classes of people, "Mr. Religion," "Mr. Friendless," and so on, to Christ.

Later in the day, Terry Winter dialogued with author Rebecca Pippert on how Christ makes a difference in a neighborhood. Pippert's description of a Christian lifestyle was as engaging as her book *Out of the Saltshaker*. The interview was skillful enough that one had the satisfied, and rare, sense of participating in it. Add the fabulous voice of Kim Wiks and you had, for my money, the finest piece of gospel TV I had seen. Too bad it is only shown at 3:00 P.M. on a Sunday. I might never have seen it had I not been put in the hospital!

Our Canadian talk-show, "One Hundred Huntley Street," caught me the same day. Once the introductory chit-chat was over, this show did not lag. Essentially it was an interview between host David Mainse and co-host Brian Stiller and family counselors Gerry and Ann Wilson. There was an excursus on our modern sexual sickness and a general chorus of thanks for Christian marriage, and pains were taken to stress that Christianity is not Victorian. There were numerous suggestions on how to make families "work," followed by prayer and the assurance that the Spirit can bring families together. Then, with the most felicitious timing, we heard a song by soprano Kathy Remple:

> O give Him all the things that hold you,
> And his Spirit like a dove
> Will descend upon your life and make you whole.[1]

"All the things that hold you"—those are the things that cause our brokenness. Giving those things to him, all of them, is the way to wholeness. I sensed the Lord's wholeness there in my hospital room.

But what of my three room-mates? Could they feel it too? They needed wholeness, I knew, especially Dominic. It seemed his family had left him along with his health. Some family members straggled in, then a girl friend and assorted visitors. The man across from me had lost his wife late in life. Over the ten days we were confined together he had no visitors. To my right, an injured police officer shared only snippets of his tough job on the downtown Street Strip.

Looking at it from their pillows, the gospel programming seemed a bit painful. It hurts to hear jubilant Christians exult in strong relationships and loving homes when all you have is brokenness, loneliness, and fear. It hurts to see well-off church-attenders sing songs of thanksgiving when you seem to have run out of blessings and have none left to count. It is good to tell such people about restoration and a new beginning. I thought—good, but not enough. Somehow we seemed too distant. It was a case of *long reach, cool touch*.

The next morning I understood what was missing. A student nurse was in for the day. Dominic was her assigned patient. As her hands nursed his hurts, she nursed his wounded spirit with soft, melodic West Indian words of forgiveness and faith. The message of forgiveness was embodied in her touch of compassion. She expressed the fullness of Christ's presence in the world, a presence that is always incarnational, always effective.

The young woman was much more than a nurse caring for the physical needs of her patient. She used the short reach and the warm touch. She became directly involved with all his needs. She gave Dominic shade in the truest sense.

That is how Christ would have each of us provide shade to "one of these brothers of mine."

Chapter 25

Let Me Hide Myself in Thee

I took an old ten-speed across southern Ontario one summer, or rather I thought I would. That leather seat made an indelible memory after about ninety miles, and so the trip was rounded off early. And the countryside was more parched than I had thought. Straggly stalks of corn stood like sparse scarecrows in ground that was too cracked and dried out even for the crows to peck on. Those are some of the painful memories. But there were many bright memories.

The trip became something of an architectural study of early Methodism in Ontario as I photographed many fine old wooden country churches that have been around for well over a century. And there was blessed relief from the sun.

One transcendent moment was a prolonged swim in the crystal clear waters of Lake Ontario near the little town of Wellington. I had been used to the more murky, badly polluted waters of the lake closer to Toronto. But out there at the tip of the Bruce Peninsula, which juts out into the lake toward Rochester, the water was a bright lime green; it was clean enough, I felt, to drink. I drank more than my share of that cold, refreshing liquid and spent a good solid hour mostly beneath the ruffled waves.

Then there were milkshakes, which my bike seemed to find on its own, and there was shade. I grew to love shade on those sunscorched roads as I had never loved shade before. Tucked in under a large dense tree, I felt life return to my limbs. Ten minutes of quality shade gives you the incredible recuperative energy you need to face the road again. It is a respite from exposure.

The suffering servant described in Isaiah 53 is the most exposed figure of the Bible. Here is one who faces the full fury of his tormentors with no shelter at all. And he faces the onslaught of his own free will:

> *I gave My back to those who struck Me,*
> *And my cheeks to those who plucked out the beard;*
> *I did not hide my face from shame and spitting. . . .*
> *I have set My face like a flint.* (Isa. 50:6–7)

What an exposed figure this is! Absolutely unsheltered from the assault he faces, he stands alone "as a root out of dry ground" (53:2), like a sheep "that is silent before its shearers" (v. 7). Images of exposure surround him. Who is this figure?

It is difficult to identify him as an Old Testament figure of Isaiah's time. As Christopher North and others show, this man cannot be the prophet Isaiah himself or one of his contemporaries.[1] Neither can the servant be Israel, even though in Isaiah the nation is often portrayed as a servant. Here, as in chapter 49, the servant's mission is to redeem his people. He is the Messiah who, as a substitute for his people, will suffer for their transgressions. Isaiah's Suffering Servant is none other than Jesus, the Christ. He is utterly exposed, not only in his passion, but in his entire life. He chose to leave the shelter of home. He was, in every sense, the exposed one, and never more so than when he would face his tormentors and hang, stripped bare, on the wooden cross. What a stark figure he is there, all the world gaping at him suspended between heaven and earth!

Yet, there is a larger truth. Christian faith rests on the fact that this is God the Son exposed to God the Father's wrath against the sins of all mankind. Our sins are placed on him as John the Baptist prophesied. The lamb of God has indeed taken away the sins of the world (see John 1:29). "The Lord has laid on him the iniquity of us all" (Isa. 53:6). He is the sin offering.

This substitution for sinners, which Isaiah portrays so vividly, is conveyed in the Christian word *atonement*. It comes from the Hebrew word *kaphar* and means "to cover," or "to cancel." *Atonement* is the covering over of transgression and the resulting reconciliation of God and man. In that sense it is helpful to break down the word to its component parts. *Atonement* is "at-one-ment." Christ's sacrifice makes us *at one* with God through penitence and faith.

Substitution is necessary for atonement. Just as it is necessary to stand between the sun and a parched object in order to provide shade, it is necessary for Christ to stand between fallen man and God's blazing wrath against sin to provide us respite and salvation. The New Testament stresses that truth. Christ is our substitute. You see, at just the right time, "while we were still helpless, Christ died for the ungodly" (Rom. 5:6). As Paul said, "Christ died for our sins, according to the Scriptures" (1 Cor. 15:3). "He made Him who knew no sin to be sin on our behalf, that we might become the righteousness of God in Him" (2 Cor. 5:21). "Christ redeemed us from the curse of the Law, having become a curse *for us*" (Gal. 3:13, italics added).

In order to fully appreciate this blessed shade, we need to reflect on all the leafy branches of the atonement. First, the atonement is a completed fact: "But now, once at the end of the ages He has appeared to put away sin by the sacrifice of Himself" (Heb. 9:26). Unlike the sacrifices of the Old Testament priesthood that had to be often repeated, this sacrifice has been offered once for all time by our great High Priest.

Second, this atonement is universal. He suffered death "crowned with glory and honor, that He, by the grace of God, might taste death for everyone" (Heb. 2:9). The shade provided here is large enough for all mankind.

Also, the atonement provides satisfactory grounds for forgiveness of sins. Anyone who runs to its shade with repentance and faith experiences peace with God: "In him we have redemption through his blood" (Eph. 1:7).

Nor is there any inadequacy or temporal limitations in the

atonement. It was in the minds of the Creator before the foundation of the world: "He was foreordained before the foundation of the world, but was manifest in these last times for you" (1 Peter 1:20). The destiny of this shade is its eternal nature.

However, universal and complete as it is the atonement does not provide universal salvation. Just as one must choose to get out of the blazing sun and rest in the coolness of shade, there is a crucial personal choice when it comes to the atonement. "He who believes and is baptized will be saved, but he who does not believe will be condemned" (Mark 16:16). John says, "He who does not believe the Son shall not see life, but the wrath of God abides on him" (John 3:36).

The sobering truth is that there is only one true shade. To miss this blessed shelter is to lose all shelter: "If we sin willfully after we have received the knowledge of the truth, there no longer remains sacrifice for sins, but a certain fearful expectation of judgment, and fiery indignation which will devour [His] adversaries" (Heb. 10:26–27).

But to pass by this shelter is unthinkable, is it not? How would it be possible? It would be like pedaling your way along the old Number Two Highway, going uphill all the way, feeling the blazing sun sap every ounce of energy from your body, and by-passing all the shade until you fall right over on the road, or sitting on the baked pavement itself, delirious in the blazing sun, until you succumb to the heat!

Ah, I remember all too well the leafy glade at the intersection of two country roads. Down at the base of a huge oak tree, with a bottle of water, I lay stretched out in the cool blades of long summer grass. The breeze dried my forehead and carried the aromas of country soil and flowers. In a place like that gradually your breath becomes more even and your heart scales down from its incessant pounding.

Goodness, the more blazing the sun, the richer the shade.

NOTES

PREFACE
   1. V. S. Naipaul, *A House for Mr. Biswas* (New York: Penguin, 1961), 302.
   2. Josef Pieper, *Leisure, the Basis of Culture* (New York: New American, 1963), 57.

CHAPTER 1
   1. Alvin Toffler, *Future Shock* (New York: Random House, 1970), 346.
   2. Toffler, 290.
   3. Toffler, 346.

CHAPTER 2
   1. Toffler, 51.
   2. Toffler, 161.
   3. Toffler, 166.
   4. Toffler, 285.
   5. John Oswalt, "The Book of Isaiah, Chapters 1–39," *New International Commentary on the Old Testament* (Grand Rapids: Eerdmans, 1986), 7.
   6. Toffler, 307.
   7. Quoted in Toffler, 308.
   8. Toffler, 324.
   9. Toffler, 323.
  10. Toffler, 322.

CHAPTER 3
   1. Toffler, 211.
   2. Jack Horn, "Bored to Sickness," *Psychology Today* (Nov. 1979), 92.
   3. Somerset Maugham, *Of Human Bondage* (Harmonsworth: Penguin, 1963), 237.
   4. Maugham, 238–9.
   5. Anne Morrow Lindbergh, *Gift From the Sea* (New York: Walker, 1984), 237.

6. Thomas à Kempis, *Of the Imitation of Christ* (New Canaan: Keats, 1973), 31–2.

PART 2

1. William Cowper, "I Am Monarch." Verses were supposedly written by Alexander Selkirk during his solitary abode on the Island of Juan Fernandez in 1782.

2. Herman Melville, *Moby Dick* (New York: W. W. Norton, 1967), 136–7.

3. Roger von Oech, *Whack on the Side of the Head* (New York: Warner Books, 1983), 32.

4. von Oech, 40.

5. von Oech, 41.

CHAPTER 4

1. Anthony Trollope, *An Autobiography* (London: Fontana, 1962), 28–9.

CHAPTER 6

1. Elisabeth Elliott, *Let Me Be A Woman* (Wheaton: Tyndale, 1976), 61.

PART 3

1. E. Howard Kerr, "Soft Falls the Snow."

CHAPTER 7

1. "O My Lovin' Brother," author unknown.

CHAPTER 8

1. Helmut Thielicke, *Christ and the Meaning of Life,* tr. J. W. Doberstein (New York: Harper and Row, 1962), 86.

2. E. Howard Kerr, "Forth From Thy Presence."

CHAPTER 9

1. Allan Bloom, *The Closing of the American Mind* (New York: Simon and Schuster, 1987), 51.

2. Bloom, 80.

CHAPTER 10

1. Bloom, 99.

2. F. W. Faber, "There's A Wideness in God's Mercy."

CHAPTER 11

1. Richard Foster, *Freedom of Simplicity* (San Francisco: Harper and Row, 1981), 95–6.

PART 4

1. Robert Bly, *The Winged Life: The Poetic Voice of Henry David Thoreau* (San Francisco: Sierra Club, 1986), 25.

2. C. S. Lewis, *Present Concerns,* ed. Walter Hooper (London: Fount, 1986), 7.

3. Bin Soto, "How Lovely Is Your Dwelling Place," from *Scripture In Song* (Auckland: Greenlane, 1979).

CHAPTER 12

1. James & Elizabeth Greenlesh, "Let There Be Glory and Honor and Praises," *Praise & Worship Songbook I* (Mobile: Integrity, 1987), 53.

2. Frances R. Havergal, "Like a River Glorious."

CHAPTER 15

1. E. Howard Kerr, "Hills."

2. George Matheson, "O Love That Wilt Not Let Me Go."

3. "How Firm a Foundation" from John Rippon's *Selection of Hymns,* 1787.

CHAPTER 16

1. Richard Foster, *The Challenge of the Disciplined Life* (San Francisco: Harper and Row, 1985), 71.

2. Foster, 71.

3. Quoted in Bly, *The Winged Life,* 58.

CHAPTER 17

1. Foster, 72.

2. Foster, 72.

3. Henry Barraclough, "Ivory Palaces."

4. Emily E. S. Elliott, "Thou Didst Leave Thy Throne."

5. Henry F. Lyte, "Abide With Me."

6. Dietrich Bonhoeffer, *Letters and Papers From Prison,* ed. Eberhard Bethge, tr. Reginald H. Fuller (London: SCM, 1953), 180–1.

7. *Calgary Herald.*

8. "I'm Just a Poor, Wayfaring Stranger," American folk hymn set to

traditional American melody from *The Singing Church* (Carol Stream, IL: Hope Publishers, 1985).

9. Robert Frost, "Stopping by Woods on a Snowy Evening."

10. Walt Whitman, "A Noiseless Patient Spider."

CHAPTER 18

1. Richard Leider, *The Power of Purpose* (New York: Ballantine, 1985), vii.

2. Matthew Arnold, "Solitude."

CHAPTER 19

1. Tom Ward, *Cowtown: An Album of Early Calgary* (Calgary: McLelland and Stewart West, 1975), 7.

2. Ward, 42.

CHAPTER 20

1. Toffler, 34.

2. E. Howard Kerr, "I'll Take the Hard Way."

3. E. Howard Kerr, "Chosen of Christ."

CHAPTER 21

1. Erich Fromm, *Escape From Freedom* (New York: Avon, 1941), 20.

CHAPTER 23

1. Albert Camus, *The Outsider,* tr. Stuart Gibert (London: Penguin Books, 1946), 13, 24.

2. Ralph Waldo Emerson, "Think Me Not Unkind."

CHAPTER 24

1. John Wimber, "The Spirit Song."

CHAPTER 25

1. Christopher North, *The Suffering Servant in Deutero-Isaiah* (Oxford: Oxford University Press, 1948), 216.

About the Author

John Charles Kerr pastors The Beddington Church in Calgary, Alberta, Canada. He is a contributing editor to *Resource,* a leadership magazine, and a writer for *Faith Today,* the voice of the Evangelical Fellowship of Canada.

He received the B.A. degree from the University of Western Ontario, the M.A. from the University of Montreal, and the M.Div. and the S.T.M. from the University of Saskatchewan.

He lives in Calgary with his wife, Ruth, and their two sons, Bob and Jeff.